Lay Ministers, Lay Disciples

LAY MINISTERS, LAY DISCIPLES

Evangelizing Power in the Parish

by

Susan Blum Gerding, Ed.D.

and

Frank P. DeSiano, C.S.P.

Paulist Press
New York/Mahwah, N.J.

Library of Congress Cataloging-in Publication Data

Gerding, Susan Blum.
Lay ministers, lay disciples : evangelizing power in the parish /
by Susan Blum Gerding and Frank P. DeSiano.
p. cm.
ISBN 0-8091-3896-4 (alk. paper)
1. Lay ministry—Catholic Church. 2. Evangelistic work.
I. DeSiano, Frank P. II. Title.
BX1916.G47 1999
253'.088'22—dc21
99-17006
CIP

Cover design by James Brisson

Published by Paulist Press
997 Macarthur Boulevard
Mahwah, New Jersey 07430

www.paulistpress.com

Printed and bound in the
United States of America

Contents

Contents

Dedication

For All Who Come behind Us

Every element of the parish must respond to the evangelical imperative—priests, religious, laypersons, staff, ministers, organizations, social clubs, parochial schools and parish religious education programs. Otherwise, evangelization will be something a few people in the parish see as their ministry—rather than the reason for the parish's existence and the objective of every ministry in the parish.

Go and Make Disciples:
A National Plan and Strategy
for Catholic Evangelization
in the United States
National Conference of Catholic Bishops, 1993

Acknowledgments

We have many people to thank; without them this book would not have been possible. In addition to our respective families, including the Paulist community, there are many lay ministers who have inspired and taught us about evangelization. They are too numerous to mention, but too wonderful to forget.

Preparation of this manuscript was helped along by the encouragement of Father Lawrence Boadt, President of Paulist Press, and Donna Crilly, editor at Paulist Press, without whose skillful eye and numerous suggestions, this manuscript might well not have survived to publication.

We are also grateful to Father Michael Driscoll, Pastor, and Mrs. Rosemary Costa Stone, Music Minister of St. Jude Parish in Boca Raton, Florida, for their invaluable pastoral and ministerial comments and suggestions.

We also extend heartfelt thanks to two wonderful churchmen, Archbishop Michael Sheehan and Bishop William Houck, who took time to read the manuscript and write, respectively, the introduction and afterword. Their dedication to evangelization and their leadership through the U.S. Bishops' Conference are stirring gifts to the church today.

INTRODUCTION

The Most Reverend Michael J. Sheehan
Archbishop of Santa Fe
Chair of the NCCB Evangelization Committee

It is a joy for me as the chairman of the U.S. Bishops'
Committee for Evangelization to highly recommend this
book, *Lay Ministers, Lay Disciples*. This book is about the
evangelizing dimensions of all parish ministries. It contains
practical helps and new ideas for receptionists and parish
secretaries, lectors, eucharistic ministers and the many other
persons who are involved in serving the people of our parishes. There are also points for reflection to review the effectiveness of the different ministers.

Evangelization means bringing the Gospel to those who
do not have a living relationship with Jesus Christ. We
often think of this as reaching out to those who have no
contact with the church—and that is certainly true.
However, there is a very important aspect of evangelization
that is much closer to us...namely, those people who are
practicing their faith minimally. Before we even think about
reaching out to those who do not have contact with the
church, we need first to ask ourselves what we are inviting

them back to. What sort of reception do they find when they come to the church? Is it easy for them to find the office? Is there a friendly, loving environment? Does the parish office desk look more inviting than a teller's window at a bank?

A great concern of mine is our outreach to the many millions of Catholics who have become inactive for whatever reason. When we send evangelizers out to knock on doors and when we make a special effort to invite the inactive back to our parishes, we must have something appealing when they return. They may have left because of indifference on the part of the priest or parish ministers. Perhaps they left because of poor liturgy, uninspired preaching or sloppy music. We must be sure that the basic elements of parish life reflect the new evangelization that Pope John Paul II is calling for. The new millennium is a time for a new way of acting, a new way of celebrating our parish life. The contents of this book will enable our parish ministers to evangelize more effectively. There is no better evangelizing method than to have a lively parish where all the ministers are conscious of their evangelizing potential. The experience of Catholic liturgy and life has an incredible appeal to people. It gives joy and energy to our regular parishioners and draws back to the fold those who have been on the margins of church life when they encounter it again.

This book will help the reader see that we must be a church of mission, not of maintenance, if we are to follow the command of Jesus to bring the Good News to all people.

CHAPTER ONE

To Advance the Story

The story of evangelization, in the wider church and in the North American church, is inevitably moving forward. We hope in writing this book to contribute to the advance of this story.

With many years of experience in evangelization on the national, diocesan and parish levels—and with thousands of frequent-flier miles behind us—we are finally finding that *evangelization* is no longer the red-flag word that it used to be in most Catholic circles. Catholics, over the thirty years in which the word *evangelization* has become part of our regular vocabulary, no longer automatically cringe when the word is uttered.

However, it can still cause a certain squeamishness, especially among some of the laity, even the growing numbers of laypersons who are active in parish ministries. We have written this book because we find that the great majority of lay ministers have difficulty realizing that they are ministers, let alone *evangelizers* as well as ministers. While some parish ministers have been enlightened through ministry formation, continuing education and consciousness-raising efforts to seek practical ways to integrate an evangelization dimension in their ministries, most are not aware of the fuller implications of their ministries—and the local churches are suffering for it.

As we advance into the third millennium, we see two specific challenges in the area of lay ministers and evangelization: first, to introduce the basics of Catholic evangelization theory and, second, to begin translating that theology and theory into practical and purposeful ministry on the parish level. This small book is written to begin addressing these two needs. Much has been written about evangelization in general on both the institutional and relational levels, but little can be found concerning the evangelizing dimension of parish ministry.

In our experience, for most lay ministers (perhaps excluding those who have completed extensive ministry formation programs) the concepts of ministry and evangelization are foreign. We find very few ushers, for instance, who would place themselves in either category. The same can be said for choir members, members of parish or finance councils, or members of the parish social justice committee. Eucharistic ministers, lectors and youth ministers may have assimilated the notion of ministry because these functions were once primarily performed by clergy; even so, probably most are not aware of the evangelization dimension within their ministries.

We have written this book because we believe in the tremendous potential of evangelization when it is applied intentionally on a practical level in *all* parish ministries. We believe this potential will bring great benefits for the church, the parish and also the individual minister.

Can we help the ushers or the choir members or the lectors in their local parishes realize the impact that evangelization can bring to their ministries, as well as to their own spiritual growth? Can we make the greeters, eucharistic ministers and youth ministers more aware of the far-reaching effects of their ministries when animated by the dimensions of evangelization developed in this book? What a more powerful church we would be if the evangelizing power of parish ministries were realized!

Using This Book

We are hopeful that this book will contribute greatly to the awareness of and interest in evangelization. We also hope that some of the practical approaches to ministry that we present will improve our expertise as a Catholic people.

Although different chapters concentrate on different ministries, together each chapter reinforces the vision, just as each ministry in the parish reinforces the entire evangelizing effort of the parish. While a particular lay minister might concentrate on one chapter of interest, we trust that he or she will not overlook the others.

This book was designed to be used in a variety of environments: (1) private reflection—a personal study in one's own area of ministry; (2) small groups—a viable resource for groups of particular ministers in a continuing education or ministry formation format; and (3) administration/staff—a comprehensive overview of the evangelization potential of all ministries on the parish and diocesan levels. Material for personal reflection at the end of each chapter will provide the individual or groups with an opportunity to identify areas of strength and weakness in ministry.

We are well aware that many ministries are not discussed in this book simply due to space limitations—ministry to the disabled, separated and divorced, young adults, various cultural groups; ministry by Catholic teachers, professional groups, altar guilds, men's clubs, Knights of Columbus and so forth. Even though we could not touch on all of these areas—but concerned ourselves with the most basic and visible parish ministries—it is our hope that all parish ministers can read this book and apply the various suggestions "where the shoe fits."

As we explore the evangelizing dimension of so many parish ministries, it might look like a glaring omission not to have included a chapter on the ministry of the evangelization team. We thought a long time about this. Our conclusion? That much has already been written for evangelization teams, both in official church documents and by various practitioners in the field. We also felt that many committed members of evangelization teams in Catholic parishes could feel patronized by our devoting a chapter to them. After all, since our main purpose is to raise the evangelization perspective for parish ministers, should we not presume that evangelization teams already have a deep evangelizing perspective?

Our suspicion, though, is that the evangelization teams will be the first ones to read this book and use it to expand their own thinking on evangelization. We look for that time when Catholics on evangelization teams will be able to put together their own book describing and explaining their own experience for the rest of the parish. With time and more ministerial maturity, that day is coming.

Before we explore the enormous potential latent in parish ministries, it will be helpful to sketch a bit of the history of the evangelization movement. Besides helping lay ministers situate themselves in the larger story of evangelization, the ups and downs of Catholic attitudes toward evangelization, even on the official level, can help explain some of the reasons why lay ministers do not readily think of themselves as evangelizers.

The Larger Story

A renewed interest in Catholic evangelization has been occurring since 1975 as the direct result of the publication of Pope Paul VI's *Evangelii Nuntiandi* (On Evangelization in the Modern World, USCC, 1975, Publication #129-26). Surely the church had cultivated, often heroically, a keen missionary vision well before this date. Its history can arguably be seen as a history of mission. But Pope Paul's message did something startling—it began to locate mission energy not simply in faraway places but, through a comprehensive perspective, in all the aspects of church life.

When Pope Paul wrote, "Evangelization is in fact the grace and vocation proper to the church, her deepest identity," the Catholic community began to hear a call to a new self-understanding. When Paul continued his thought by saying, "[The church] exists in order to evangelize, that is to say, in order to preach and teach, to be the channel of the gift of grace, to reconcile sinners with God, and to perpetuate Christ's sacrifice in the mass, which is the memorial of his death and glorious resurrection," he challenged every Catholic, and every minister, to rethink his or her role (*Evangelii Nuntiandi*, #14).

Paul divided his historic apostolic exhortation into seven chapters that show the breadth of his thinking. The first chapter related Christ to his community, the perfect Evangelizer to the evangelizing church. The second chapter sketched a penetrating and broad definition of evangelization, and the third focused on the content of the church's message. While chapter four reviewed the methods of evangelization and called for new methods corresponding to our modern technology, the fifth chapter broke new ground. In this chapter, Paul reviewed all the beneficiaries of evangelization and included in his list even the baptized, even those already evangelized. This vision made spreading and living the Gospel the agenda of every baptized person, and made clear the need for ongoing evangelization throughout a Christian's life. The final two chapters talked about the workers of evangelization—quite deliberately highlighting clergy, religious and laypeople—and the hope-filled spirit that has to accompany this often-difficult ministry.

Even *National Catholic Reporter* columnist Arthur Jones, occasionally an outspoken critic, wrote:

> Paul VI's superb, tightly reasoned, 23,000-word exhortation grappled with the difficult task of describing what evangelization is and insisted that presenting the gospel is not an optional contribution for Catholics. The Christian community's responsibility toward humanity was contained in a message that could equally be warmly received by fundamentalist charismatics or liberation theology proponents but not equally easily rejected. (*NCR*, August 20, 1979, 44)

The story advanced further when Pope John Paul II coined the term *new evangelization* while giving a speech in the Dominican Republic in 1983 (*Origins*, March 24, 1983, 661); he has used or referred to that term ("a new springtime of evangelization") in nearly every talk he has given or document he has written since then. As an example, his recent document on preparing for the third millennium, *Tertio Millennio Adveniente* (*Origins*, November 24, 1994), stressed the need for evangelization and ongoing conversion of all people.

Even with this energetic start and strong papal push, not all bishops, clergy or laity shared the vision or enthusiasm for lay involvement in Catholic evangelization. The support of the U.S. bishops as a body has often been enthusiastic, but, like that of most busy ministers in the church today, also sometimes hard to maintain at a high level. Other concerns have sometimes in the past made them put evangelization, despite their intentions and words, lower on their priority list, both as a conference and in the local dioceses. Not only have the bishops had difficulty keeping Paul VI's sharp focus—the tendency is systemic throughout church life.

However, by 1977, the U.S. bishops, through their conference, the NCCB, had established an Ad Hoc Committee on Evangelization and appointed Rev. Alvin A. Illig, C.S.P., as its executive director. Simultaneously, Father Illig and the Paulist community founded the Paulist National Catholic Evangelization Association, and with the endorsement of the bishops, produced several national celebrations of lay evangelization from which many of today's contemporary evangelizers received their initial inspiration.

While agreeing publicly that evangelization was their responsibility, some bishops appeared to pay lip service to the notion that evangelization was a "normative" right and responsibility for lay Catholics. The very word *evangelization* struck discordant notes among some of the bishops, as it also did with most clergy and laity at that time. For example, to pass on an anecdotal reference, in 1980, one of the bishops was questioned in a letter from a layperson regarding Pope Paul VI's universal call to evangelization for all believers.

The query was based on *Evangelii Nuntiandi* and quoted the great commission of Jesus at the end of Matthew (28:19–20). The bishop responded by returning the letter, writing in the margin of the letter that this particular scripture passage was "reserved only for the episcopate."

Fortunately, other bishops did not agree with this interpretation. In that same year, for instance, Archbishop Edward McCarthy, known nationally as one of the earliest supporters of the Catholic evangelization movement in the United States, established one of the first evangelization councils in the country, consisting of bishops, priests, women religious and, pointedly, laypeople. By 1985 he had developed through his council a five-year plan for evangelization in the Archdiocese of Miami, which included the hiring of one of the first full-time directors of evangelization in the country—a laywoman. Not only were bishops becoming more committed to the idea, but they were also demonstrating the place of laypeople in the spread of Christ's message.

Like Archbishop McCarthy, other bishops have learned the value and necessity of delegation and "reproduction"— the pastoral process by which others come to share in the universal missionary mandate that lies at the heart of each bishop's mandate. This, of course, is what the great commission is based upon—"Go and make disciples..." so that they can go and make disciples...so that they can go and make disciples... (see Mt 28:19).

However, lay involvement was often regarded with some suspicion (perhaps rightly) as Catholic evangelization programs emerged that were directly modeled on Protestant home visitation ministries or church growth programs. Catholics in these early years saw themselves very much as novices in the movement, borrowing what they could. Still, the very existence of these efforts spoke of the growth of an evangelizing consciousness among the laypeople of the church. Since not many pastors were willing or able to assume the responsibility of training and guiding laypeople interested in evangelization, few parish evangelization committees existed through the eighties and well into the early nineties. As a result, Catholic lay evangelizers sought training and formation wherever they could find it.

Meanwhile, the need for evangelization continued to grow stronger and more obvious on all fronts: Large numbers of Catholics were leaving the flock to join evangelical churches—or just plain leaving. Others, in a highly mobile society in which 10 percent of the population moved each year, were not reconnecting with a local parish, thereby forming another source of active Catholics "leaving" the church. Those who did not physically leave the church through a geographical move or through formal disassociation left in their own quiet way, as declining mass attendance showed. Also of great concern were the growing rates of abortion and divorce, the increasing legion of single mothers and the numbers of young people leaving the church once they were confirmed. The influx of new peoples into the United States, particularly Latinos and Asians, also brought new opportunities and challenges. The breadth of Paul VI's vision of evangelization as a ministry for all has proven prophetic in the light of post-Vatican II pastoral developments.

The need for evangelization continued to grow so strong and obvious on all fronts that more and more Catholic laity started taking interest, even, at times, in direct disobedience to their pastors. A common complaint of lay evangelizers even in the late eighties was, "My pastor told me that I am not allowed to evangelize."

However, there were always reasons for optimism. One positive event occurred in 1983: the creation, with the support of the bishops, of the National Council for Catholic Evangelization. This organization, while independent of the bishops in a formal sense, actually serves as a network of laypeople, religious and priests involved in or interested in evangelization. A large part of their membership presently consists of diocesan personnel—clergy and lay-persons—in charge of evangelization.

For many years, though, this organization was one of the lone voices, along with the Paulist National Catholic Evangelization Association, attempting to awake the American church to the call of evangelization. In spite of the rhetoric and some optimistic signs, by 1990 only a handful of the nineteen thousand parishes in the United States, and less than a handful of the 189 dioceses had established full-time evangelization offices or volunteer committees chaired by full-time professional ministers. Father Illig, who had traveled tirelessly to buttress the cause, predicted in the seventies that "DPEs (directors of primary evangelization) would be as prevalent and as common as DREs in parishes." By the early nineties, this had not come close to fulfillment.

What has changed the climate of the recent church in its attitudes toward evangelization?

In response to many factors, the U.S. bishops in 1993 issued a powerful document on evangelization, *Go and Make Disciples: A National Plan and Strategy for Catholic Evangelization in the United States*, with a nearly unanimous vote. Many of the earliest evangelizers were astounded that the bishops offered such a strong and united affirmation of Catholic evangelization. The vision of Paul VI was taking deeper root.

The bishops proposed three major goals, each of which offers a striking way in which to think of the ministry of the parish, and of laypersons who serve the parish as ministers. The goals that the bishops put forth reinforce the challenge that springs from making evangelization a priority:

1. To bring about in all Catholics such an enthusiasm for their faith that, in living their faith in Jesus, they freely share it with others;

2. To invite all people in the United States, whatever their social or cultural background, to hear the message of salvation in Jesus Christ so they may come to join us in the fullness of the Catholic faith;

3. To foster gospel values in our society, promoting the dignity of the human person, the importance of the family and the common good of our society, so that our nation may continue to be transformed by the saving power of Jesus Christ.

As a result of *Go and Make Disciples*, the story of the nineties in the U.S. Catholic family has been one of growing awareness, greater interest and more expertise in all the aspects of evangelization. This is where we believe we are today.

As the story of evangelization continues to unfold in the church and in our personal lives as Catholics, we hope the reflections in this book advance the story of living and sharing the Good News of Jesus Christ. We hope our efforts will make this story all the more compelling, particularly for those men and women who set aside time weekly or daily to bring Christ, through their parish, to today's world.

CHAPTER TWO

Parish Ministry: The Laity and Evangelization

The church is not truly established and does not fully live,
nor is she a perfect sign of Christ among people,
unless there exists a laity worthy of the name,
working alongside the hierarchy,
for the Gospel cannot be deeply imprinted
on the mentality, life and work of any people
without the active presence of lay people.
Vatican II, *Ad Gentes*, #21

"I could not believe it," the woman's voice spoke through the phone. She explained that, after years of being uninvolved in the church, she decided to attend Good Friday services at a downtown parish in the center of the city. "There were women giving out Holy Communion," she continued. "I never would have believed it. How long has this been happening?"

The shock of this woman reconnecting with her church shows the dramatic changes that have happened in expanding the roles of ministry in the church since the Second Vatican Council. Even the most casual observer sees that opportunities for ministry abound for laypeople in the church today. The laity are, first, performing ministerial tasks and services once reserved for the clergy. Can you imagine women, or men, distributing communion back in 1962? Or laypersons serving as lectors, proclaiming the Word of God in the days when altar servers moved books from one side of the altar to the other?

It goes even further. We now identify services that used to be routinely provided by the laity (and sometimes were taken for granted) as formal ministries. The women of the altar society, who cleaned the church and decorated it for special occasions, are now ministers of the environment— as are others who care for the physical parish plant, including architects, painters and maintenance men. Secretaries and clerical assistants are now seen as greeters or ministers of hospitality. Those who used to visit the sick in their neighborhoods are now ministers to the sick, and those who used to console mourners are now called ministers to the bereaved. Ministry—and particularly ministry by laypeople—has become very visible today.

Look at what happens routinely in a parish. Greeters welcome, ministers of song help lead the singing, lectors proclaim the sacred scriptures, catechists accompany those preparing for baptism, eucharistic ministers help distribute the consecrated bread and wine. Very probably, youth ministers are organizing some activities for the week. This is the way our Catholic Church now looks every Sunday.

The great variety of ministries available for lay men and women today is largely due to the emerging role of the laity as a result of Vatican II. Before, *ministry* was a narrowly defined term usually limited exclusively to the ordained ministry of the episcopate or the presbyterate and occasionally extended to consecrated men and women serving the church in official capacities. In the pre-Vatican II days even "permanent deacons" were virtually a fantasy. And, of course, the laity exercised a passive role.

In the seventies and eighties, however, the concept of ministry was broadened considerably: first, to include members of the church acting in the name of the local faith community and, eventually, to all the services performed in faith by the members of the community as individuals in their public and private life as well as members acting in the name of the local church community.

This much broader definition is totally inclusive and identifies all baptized Christians as called to ministry. Catholic theologian Richard McBrien succinctly contrasted these two extreme views of ministry—the notion that ministry is restricted to the ordained and the notion that everyone is regarded as called to ministry by baptism: "The first extreme is outdated; the second not yet fully challenged" (*Catholicism*, HarperCollins, vol. 2, p. 842).

Unfortunately, due perhaps to this broadening of the concept, the very meaning of the word *ministry* has become ambiguous. Like *love*, it has come to have many meanings through misuse and overuse; in fact, it can mean almost anything to anyone, ranging from the ministry of the ordained (bishops, priests and deacons), to designated lay ministry specifically authorized by the church (eucharistic ministers, lectors), to all Christian service (corporal and spiritual acts of mercy), and to all service in general (even, one fears, to smiling and saying, "Have a nice day!").

However much these notions of ministry expand, evolve and become more clearly defined, two things are undeniable: (1) ministry is here to stay; and (2) if the church is to grow and thrive in the third millennium, that ministry, whether ordained or lay, had better be evangelizing ministry.

In fact, the approach of the church today is to understand its very essence as an evangelizing community. Consequently, the more clearly that ministry is rooted in the mission of the church as bringer of Good News to the world and harbinger of the kingdom, the more effective it will be.

Ministry and Evangelization

What does evangelization have to do with ministry? Let's explore this a bit.

In 1980, the U. S. bishops affirmed the right and responsibility of laypeople to minister in their document on lay ministry, *Called and Gifted:* "Baptism and confirmation empower all believers to share in some form of ministry....[T]hrough baptism and confirmation lay men and women have been given rights and responsibilities to participate in the mission of the church."

Fifteen years later (1995) in *Called and Gifted for the Third Millennium*, the bishops reaffirmed the role of the laity in ministry, once again urging laypeople to attend to the four "calls" of lay ministry: "...to holiness, to community, to mission and ministry, and to adulthood/Christian maturity."

Pope John Paul II has written extensively of laypeople and their various roles in the church and the world. He says, "Pastors, therefore, ought to acknowledge and foster the ministries, the offices and roles of the lay faithful that find their foundation in the sacraments of baptism and confirmation, indeed, for a good many of them, in the sacrament of matrimony" (*Christifideles Laici*, #23). He goes on to specify the place of the parish in this ministry: "The ecclesial community...finds its most immediate and visible expression in the parish. It is there that the church is seen locally. In a certain sense it is the church living in the midst of the homes of her sons and daughters" (#26).

The logic is clear: baptism and confirmation bring us into the living community of Jesus Christ—a community where faith is instilled, nourished, challenged and deepened—a community that embodies itself, in the experience of most Catholics, in their local parish. The parish, then, becomes a locus of evangelization. Or, to say it another way, parishes are communities of the evangelized called to evangelize further.

We can understand this in theological and in practical ways. Theologically, Catholics experience faith in community. In no way do Catholics see themselves as being individually "zapped" by some divine impulse that does not bear on their relationship to Christ's community of faith. In baptism, we are washed together; in the eucharist, we are fed together. When the Word is proclaimed, it is done out loud, so that hearing it together, we are further formed as God's people. While this hardly means that Catholics do not have deep personal experiences of faith—indeed, they do—it does mean that our personal experience is always in the context of our being members of Jesus Christ, called around his table and called to get up from the table to serve others in faith. So when we Catholics evangelize, it is always as members of a community grounded in baptism

19

and eucharist; and when we invite, we invite people to discover the Jesus who continues to live in his community, the church. Parishes form a fundamental part of this discovery.

The place of the parish has some very practical meanings as well. The U.S. bishops, for example, addressing evangelization, wrote in *Go and Make Disciples: A National Plan and Strategy for Catholic Evangelization in the United States:*

> Every element of the parish must respond to the evangelical imperative—priests, religious, laypersons, staff, ministers, organizations, social clubs, parochial schools and parish religious education programs. Otherwise, evangelization will be something a few people in the parish see as their ministry—rather than the reason for the parish's existence and the objective of every ministry in the parish.

The evangelical imperative extends directly to the life and ministry of the parish.

How, then, do we unlock the evangelizing potential of our parishes and the evangelizing potential of all those who do ministries in our parishes? This is an essential pastoral project for today's church.

Millions of people currently serve the people of God, the church, as ministers, both in official and unofficial ways. Most of the official ministers in the church such as priests, deacons, women religious, directors of religious education, youth ministers, choir directors and so forth are full-time, salaried, degreed or accredited ministers. Because they have such an extensive commitment to the service of the church as ministers, it is possible that they will be aware of their roles as evangelizing ministers. (It is also possible that these professionals themselves overlook the evangelizing dimension of their work.) However, many of the nonprofessional, volunteer, part-time ministers, though trained in specific areas of ministry, may not have the slightest clue to the evangelizing dimension of ministry.

These volunteer lay ministers usually serve in specific areas of ministry, for example, as eucharistic ministers and lectors; ministers to the sick, the grieving, the separated and divorced; and even in various roles that perhaps are not usually recognized as "ministries"—serving as ushers, welcoming committee members, parish council or finance committee members, office receptionists and clerical workers, janitors and maintenance personnel...or even parishioners raising funds for the parish through some common project. For many Catholic laypeople, knowing they are ministers seems foreign enough, let alone knowing they are evangelizing ministers.

A good example of this might be a couple who facilitates engaged encounters in their parish. The content of their ministry is "marriage preparation," but, when looked at closely, is not the work of their ministry evangelization? They obviously lead couples through discussions on finances or family planning as they prepare young couples for marriage; but, more importantly, they are serving as evangelizing ministers. Through their welcoming, encouraging, forming and strengthening new disciples who will bring about dimensions of the kingdom of God in their homes, they are making the Good News real. From their homes, the newly married will radiate the presence of Christ in their neighborhoods, to their friends, to today's world. When the day is over, it is not merely the content of their program that the engaged couples will remember; it is the witness of the married couple, their faith, their fidelity, that will have the greatest impact, gospel impact.

Our hope, then, is that with additional training or formation, the consciousness of all ministers can be raised so they can see their service in light of their primary role as evan-geliers. Pope Paul VI said it very well: "Modern man listens more willingly to witnesses than to teachers, and if he does listen to teachers, it is because they are witnesses" (*Evangelii Nuntiandi*, #41).

What It Means to Be a Minister

What is it that distinguishes ministry from service in general? Further, what is it that makes ministry evangelizing?

The one decisive element that distinguishes ministry from ordinary acts of kindness is motivation, and the motivation singularly necessary for ministry is discipleship. Discipleship is the foundation of ministry; one cannot be a minister if one is not first a disciple. Christian ministry and service—all Christian good works—flow out of the relationship that one has with Jesus Christ, Son of the living God. A minister is a follower of Christ. A minister lives the life of Christ. A minister follows his teachings. A minister follows his way. A minister follows his example. A minister continues his deeds.

Let's see what this means in a little more detail. To be a follower of Christ is, first of all, to "put on the mind of Christ," as St. Paul says in his letter to the Philippians (2:6). This means that the beatitudes—those constitutional statements of Christian joy—become our personal consciousness (see Mt 5:1 ff.). These are attitudes of total trust (not being afraid of being poor, of knowing how to weep, of putting our own pride aside) and also attitudes of profound service (seeking peace, working for justice and righteousness, being willing to suffer for the sake of the kingdom of God). We cannot minister without total trust in God, from whom all grace freely comes, and without a willingness to put ourselves aside in service to others.

Putting on the mind of Christ entails, secondly, that we be willing to engage the process by which this happens—the process of dying and rising that is at the heart of all Christian experience. In the Letter to the Romans (6:3 ff.), St. Paul says that our baptisms mean exactly that: We have died with Christ and, by our way of life, have begun to rise with Christ. In this, he echoes Christ's own words that unless we are willing to die, we cannot experience life (e.g., Mk 8:34–35). This opens up a whole way for us to understand Christian ministry *as those actions that help us in the process of dying and rising in Christ.*

Dying and rising, after all, happen throughout life on multiple levels. Any true growth means death and resurrection. Any commitment. Any sacrifice done from our hearts. Any selfless service. Any act of education or consolation or encouragement or counseling—all of these actions, at their root, involve dying and rising.

How powerfully this fits in with our Catholic experience, which celebrates the death and resurrection of Jesus at the heart of our worship and spirituality. Every Sunday we gather to celebrate and proclaim: "Christ has died, Christ is risen, Christ will come again." The Easter Triduum, our basic feast, is a three-day sacramental reinvolvement in the death and resurrection of Christ. Baptism, marriage, reconciliation, healing—these sacraments all point to the dying and rising that constitute our Christian life. And these sacraments, along with preparation for them and living their implications, all ground the various ministries that we do.

Another basic attitude that is necessary for ministry is gratitude—thanksgiving. How significant that our Sunday worship is also called *eucharist*—from the Greek word for thanksgiving. Because ministers, like Mary the Mother of God, are grateful for the "great things God has done" (Lk 1:49), they will serve others in God's name and with God's spirit of gentleness, compassion, forgiveness, healing and empowerment. Is it any wonder that St. Paul urges his congregations to "give thanks at all times" (1 Thes 5:18)?

Reverse Directions

To understand what it means to be a minister, we might reverse the direction and pose a few questions about being on the receiving end of ministry: "When has someone ministered to me? What were the circumstances? What, specifically, did the minister do? Was it helpful? How did it feel? Who is this person who touched my life through ministry? How did this person bring God's Good News?"

Case: Claire and Jim have just moved with their family from California to New Jersey and attend their first mass at their new parish. They are welcomed by a greeter in the vestibule. He then makes a point of introducing them to a few other families whom he knows live in their new neighborhood. After mass he introduces them to the pastor and a few more parishioners and then gives them a tour of the church and the school. He leaves them with a genuine feeling that they are very welcome in this parish, mentioning that he will call them to see how else he and his wife can help them settle into their new community. Claire and Jim felt relieved. They have been welcomed to Christ's table.

Case: Mildred is a young widow who has just gone through the shocking and traumatic experience of burying her husband, the victim of a yearlong struggle with cancer. Throughout the ordeal before his death, many friends and neighbors brought meals for her family and just spent time with her, listening, praying and trying to help in any way possible. These same neighbors organized a reception after the funeral, providing refreshments for the grieving family and the hundreds of mourners. Mildred is grateful. She has received the consolation of Christ.

Case: A young engaged couple turns to the parish for marriage preparation. After making them wait for nearly an hour, the person in charge of marriage preparation rudely dismisses the couple upon learning that they have been living together. They are angry. They have not felt Christ's love.

Case: The father of a suicide victim confides all of the details of his son's death to a member of the parish bereavement committee. In turn, she spreads the news to anyone who will listen, and soon the entire community knows all about these private and privileged details. Now he hurts even more. He has not felt Christ's trust.

Obviously, these circumstances provide a wide range and variety of possibilities in ministry (or nonministry). In the positive cases, ministry is effective, caring and life-giving. In the negative cases, however, theactions become destructive and result in pain, anger, alienation.

The positive examples point out some vital and universal dimensions of effective ministry rooted in a sense of discipleship that would apply across the board in all ministries: hospitality, listening skills, sincere caring and concern for the person, practical assistance and helpfulness, confidentiality, compassion, acceptance, patience, extending oneself, going out of one's way for another person.

It is discipleship, then, that distinguishes ministry from just plain service or charity. It is discipleship that makes our actions effective deeds that partake in the salvation of Christ. We truly minister when we consciously and intentionally help others as disciples with a sense of gratitude in the name and power and love of Jesus Christ.

Six Vital Dimensions of Evangelizing Ministers

Now, having distinguished between ministry and service, what makes ministry evangelizing? Quite simply this: recognizing that the salvation Christ has given us can be powerfully communicated to and shared with others through our ministry.

Utilizing the same characteristics of a disciple mentioned above, evangelizing ministers go one step further and share their faith with others. An evangelizing minister not only is a follower of Christ but also invites others to follow Christ. An evangelizing minister not only lives the life of Christ but also invites others to live that life. An evangelizing minister not only follows the teachings of Jesus but also invites others to follow. The pattern is clear: what we have received, so we give; as we give, so we will receive (cf. Mt 10:8).

Several vital dimensions or requirements form the character of an effective evangelizing minister: discipleship, friendship (love), witness, proclamation, invitation and integration.

Discipleship, the first requirement for ministry, is also the dominant prerequisite for effective evangelization from which all of the other dimensions flow. Discipleship is a "given" for an evangelizing minister; a person cannot be an evangelizing minister unless he or she is first a disciple. It is impossible to share faith with others if you do not possess it yourself.

Second, evangelizing ministers are *truly interested* in the welfare and concerns of people. They do not look at a person as a "prospect" (as some would-be evangelists might) but place the care and love for that person first. An evangelizing minister is open to forming new, all-inclusive friendships, welcoming the stranger in his neighborhood, parish or workplace.

Third, evangelizing ministers *witness* to their faith both verbally and nonverbally through their words and actions. People do not have any problem identifying where evangelizing ministers stand; their faith is evident and consistent in both communication and behavior, in what they say and in what they do, in how they love and in how they live their lives. As witnesses, their faith is silently implied as the reason for the way they live.

Fourth, evangelizing ministers go beyond witness to also *proclaim* their faith explicitly in Jesus. They never assume that people know that their faith, their personal relationship with and commitment to God, is the reason, the motivating factor, behind their acts of service. As proclaimers, though, they are not pushy or aggressive in sharing the source of their faith; they are gentle and graceful ministers of evangelization.

Evangelizing ministers *invite*, always encouraging others to grow, to experience God in a deeper, more profound, more intimate way. They continually draw people to conversion—ongoing conversion—from wherever they are in their faith journeys. Not only do they share their faith and faith experiences, but also encourage others to consider, celebrate or correct their own paths, their own journeys. (Of course, only the Holy Spirit can convert people's hearts and minds, so evangelizing ministers cannot convert anyone, but they are facilitators of conversion.)

Finally, evangelizing ministers are not *"lone rangers";* they always operate out of a community of believers. Their long-term goal is to introduce and integrate others into the heart of that community in whatever ways are appropriate. Their desire is to form others into disciples so that they may go out to befriend others, witness their faith, proclaim their faith, invite others into deeper relationships with God and integrate them into vibrant, loving faith communities as new disciples...so that they may, in turn, go out. Evangelization is cyclical, as Pope Paul VI wrote: "[T]he person who has been evangelized goes on to evangelize others" (*Evangelii Nuntiandi* #24).

This evangelizing dimension of ministry provides an important measure against which we can measure the ministries of our parishes. Do our ministers have the "mind of Christ" and freely display the attitudes that make their ministry explicitly evangelizing? Each one of us involved in ministry might examine his or her heart in the light of what it means to be "called and gifted" as ministers who evangelize.

Have I Told You Lately That I Love You?

For more than two decades, whether at a large stadium rally, a parish confirmation service or in a personal, one-on-

one conversation, Archbishop Edward McCarthy, the former Archbishop of Miami, regularly asked his flock the question from the popular song, "Have I told you lately that I love you?"

The question might well haunt each one of us, as Jesus Christ asks each of his followers, "Have I told you lately that I love you?"

As ministers seek to evangelize in the spirit of sincerely inviting others into a deeper, more intimate relationship with Jesus Christ, we become "his hands, his feet, his voice." Through us, Jesus asks others, "Have I told you lately that I love you?"

This question grounds the foundational attitude of the evangelizing lector proclaiming the Word of God, the evangelizing eucharistic minister administering the cup, the evangelizing choir member praising God in song, the evangelizing usher welcoming the stranger, the evangelizing hunger committee member. The same question is asked through the neighbor who prepares meals for someone recuperating from surgery or through the businessman who everyone knows can be trusted.

In so many ways, through ministry, our lips are the lips of Christ saying to people in today's world, "Have I told you lately that I love you":

The recent widow who is grateful for the visit from a member of her parish, who not only helped to meet her immediate needs but assisted in planning the funeral and gave long-term care in the lonely months after the funeral.

The members of a small rural community who are grateful for the trained layperson who has accepted the responsibility of providing communion services in her parish when the "circuit priest" is serving in one of his seven other churches.

The divorcee who is deeply touched by the sensitivity of a peer minister who enters into her pain, disappointment and sense of failure.

The young, single mother who rejoins the church after realizing that she is neither being condemned nor judged by the parish staff member who arranges baptismal preparation for her infant daughter.

Our lives are touched by a variety of ministries, ordained and lay, full-time and part-time, salaried and volunteer, both in church and out: the Catholic doctor who prays with us before surgery; the parents and grandparents who care for us; the teacher who inspires us; the priest who encourages us; the spouse who loves us; the bishop who leads us; the coworker who brings us cookies on Valentine's day; the neighbor who cares for our Alzheimer-afflicted spouse for an afternoon; the eucharistic minister who brings holy communion when we are sick.

If the basic mission of the church is to evangelize, then every ministry must, by definition, be an evangelizing ministry. It is our contention that if a ministry is not an evangelizing ministry, then the existence of the ministry itself must be questioned and challenged, redefined and transformed. Evangelization is not just an *item* on the agenda of any parish or any ministry; evangelization is *the* agenda. Evangelization in this way is much more than a specific ministry; it becomes a Catholic way of life. It becomes the way for Christ to say that he continues loving us today.

Reflecting on Our Ministry

• How did I get involved in my ministry? What was my motive?

• How do I experience myself as evangelizing in my ministry and my daily life?

• When do I most experience myself as a disciple? How does being a disciple make me feel in terms of my responsibilities to others, to the church, to God?

• How would I describe myself as a witness to Jesus Christ?

• What opportunities can I identify for proclaiming my faith in Christ?

• Do I invite people to faith tactfully, with respect, with care for their needs?

• Do I sense myself as deeply connected to the parish community, drawing my spiritual energy from the parish's worship and life? Do I invite people to experience Christ in his community?

• When was the last time I was an opportunity for another person to learn that Jesus loves him or her?

CHAPTER THREE

Hospitality: The Heart of Evangelization Receptionists, Greeters and Ushers

Let mutual love continue.
Do not neglect to show hospitality to strangers,
for by doing that some have
entertained angels without knowing it.
Hebrews 13:1–2, NRSV

Like most members of the parish, many ministers of hospitality—receptionists, greeters and ushers—probably do not consider themselves as either ministers or evangelizers. Yet, in his historic document on evangelization, *Evangelii Nuntiandi*, Pope Paul VI invited everyone—the whole church—to evangelize. Upon reflection, these ministers of hospitality, who really serve as "gatekeepers," can come to see themselves as specially poised to evangelize.

Many Catholics today would eagerly acknowledge that eucharistic ministers, lectors and altar servers who serve during mass qualify as lay ministers. However, many receptionists, greeters and ushers would probably resist putting the label "ministry" on what they do. Many would also reject the idea that they are called to be evangelizers.

When this notion is suggested, they resist fearfully, "Who? Me? An evangelizer?" The suggestion is challenged by comments such as, "Do I have to preach on street corners? Do I have to knock on doors?" They conclude, "No, I'm not an evangelizer. I'm just a receptionist! Just an usher! Just a greeter!" In this they echo the instinctive reaction of most Catholics, which comes from the same common lack of knowledge of how the Gospel is lived and spread.

While these ministers don't have to knock on doors or preach on street corners, as "gatekeepers," they do have a marvelous opportunity to evangelize as they set a tone, an aura of hospitality, a sense of welcome, in the parishes in which they serve. They can be the hands, the feet, the voice of Jesus, welcoming and serving his friends. "Come unto Me," Jesus says to people through the voice of the gatekeepers. "All who are weary and troubled will find rest" (Mt 11:28).

Receptionists

As ushers and greeters serve as the "doorkeepers" in church, so the parish receptionist serves in the rectory when people call or visit for particular purposes during the week. Just as ushers and greeters, along with other ministers, set the tone for the church, so the receptionist plays an essential role in setting the tone for those who approach the church offices.

If, that is, they can even find the church offices! One of our key tests for a welcoming parish is our ability, upon arriving at a parish we have not visited before, to feel oriented and served. The third or fourth time one walks around the grounds or drives around the block looking for an open door or a human being seals one's impression that the parish may care a lot about itself, but it doesn't give a whit about its people or visitors.

In this vein, a true story is told of an inactive Catholic who had finally been convinced to go back to church after an absence of some thirty years. He had read a newspaper article about a particularly lively church in his city and decided to accept the invitation for all inactive Catholics to give the church a "second chance." He called the church receptionist, who gave him excellent instructions for reaching the church and then told him that the meeting for inactive Catholics would be in the school library. Arriving at the parish, he had no idea which of the several buildings was the school, but he saw a sign that said "N.A. Meeting" with a directional arrow. He followed the signs and was amazed at the extremely warm welcome he received from everyone in the room. Everybody was so glad to see him and welcomed him for his first time at the meeting. Shortly after the meeting began, he realized that "N.A." did not mean "nonactive," as he had presumed. As one after the other stood and introduced themselves, "Hi! I'm John! And I'm a crack addict," or "Hi! I'm Jane, and I'm a heroin addict," he realized his mistake. He was at a Narcotics Anonymous meeting!

When it was his turn to introduce himself, he admitted his mistake and turned to leave. Several members of the group tried to stop him, assuring him that he was so very welcome that they wanted him to join their group. "We all know how difficult it is to come for the very first time!" they assured him. "Are you sure you don't want to stay? We really want to help you."

The meeting room for inactive Catholics was not well marked, and this particular gentleman never returned to the church again. True story. One wonders if he would have been so well received and warmly welcomed at other meetings.

"Push 1 if..."

Receptionists are the first level of that "inner presence" of a parish, the one that serves as the center for ministry in a parish. They are, obviously, the voice of the parish, creating the very first impression people get when they call with a question or a need. While most businesses today have turned to voice mail, with a synthesized voice directing the caller to hit one or another phone button, many other businesses know that having a friendly person respond to a call can make the difference between a sale and a disgruntled customer.

Parishes, many of which are also turning to electronic reception services, run even a greater risk—of making someone feel dismissed. The current joke concerning church voice mail is, "Push 1 if you're going to commit suicide; push 2 if you're going to commit homicide." Calling the church is not as mundane or impersonal as calling a corporate office or a governmental unit; it deserves a personal response. Granted, some callers only want to know what time the masses are for a given Sunday or holy day, and parish phone lines often get overloaded. Perhaps a compromise would have an electronic service that said, "If you want mass times or directions to the church, press 1....Otherwise, stay on the line and your call will be taken as soon as possible." Instead of a long list of options for various extensions, a real person will answer the call. While each parish faces different demands in communication, the test for successfully serving the public should be the friendly access and welcome a stranger would receive.

In many parishes the responsibilities of the receptionist are separate from the church secretary, but in cases where the secretary also serves as the receptionist, volunteers could be sought and trained to answer the telephone warmly and graciously, directing the calls as necessary. (Incidentally, if teenagers are used to answer the phone after school or in the evenings, be sure they are well trained in the spirit of hospitality and evangelization.)

Subtle tones of voice say, on the one hand, "We are here to serve you, thank you for calling," or on the other hand, "We are very busy and you have just intruded on our work." As a "keeper of the gate," a receptionist can communicate an openness to the caller, or the receptionist can send out vibrations that say, "We don't want to be bothered."

Inner/Outer Worlds

Receptionists are often caught between two worlds, one being a world of clergy who often have little free time, and the other being the world of an expectant and needy public. Even if the clergy or parish staff person is busy or occupied, is there ever a justification for a curt response like: "He's not in" or "She's busy" or "We can't help you"?

Receptionists, too, are also caught between an inner world of obligations that can include typing, photocopying, stamping and sealing envelopes, preparing lunch and even cleaning a rest room, and an outer, public world coming in through the phone or the front door. Caught between the two, the receptionist often naturally chooses to serve the inner world rather than the outer one. Yet, the inner world will always be there, with more letters to get out, more copies to make and more stamps to lick. The outer world, the person calling in, may be there just once, with a particular need or request that, for the caller, may mean advancing in faith or being put off from the church.

One of the key services receptionists can perform is to communicate clearly to the parish professionals the needs that are being presented, helping the staff person to interpret what is being asked. Receptionists are mediators of that important communication between seeker and servant. Much as receptionists are tempted to protect the parish professionals, they need to be just as protective of those who call in.

Receptionists know that when the phone rings, it could be someone inquiring about joining the church, an inactive parent looking to prepare a child for a sacrament, a distraught relative calling about a loved one's turn for the worse, a teen trying to connect with the parish or a parishioner desiring to give his or her time in service. Such knowledge means that all calls are potentially sacred moments, entry points to the kingdom, graced occasions that open doors and change lives.

The scriptures give us images of those times when the people around Jesus "managed" others—keeping the pesky children away (Mt 19:4) or quieting the blind man who cried out to Jesus (Mt 20:30)—and these images caution us regarding our own need to manage access to the parish. Certainly, calls need to be screened and requests need to be sorted. But, before any of this, people need to be served.

Parishes should regularly inventory the reception ministry of the parish to make sure that it is responsive to the mission, vision and ministry that is at the heart of the parish community.

Greeters

Like receptionists extending hospitality in the church office, greeters at mass also affect the tone and worship in a parish. Greeters can make an enormous difference in the way a person feels upon entering a church for mass, especially a newcomer or guest who is attending for the very first time.

The function and style of greeters, or the welcoming committee, as they are called in some parishes, varies from church to church and even geographically from region to region. Members and visitors at Southern and Midwestern churches are graciously welcomed by the greeters, whereas sometimes Northeastern or New England greeters are a little more reserved.

Regardless of the style, though, one characteristic is critical in the ministry of hospitality: the sincerity and warmth of the parish. Does a genuine sense of hospitality exist in the parish? Do the people in the pews really care whether newcomers, visitors or strangers come? Are new members authentically desired and welcomed in various parish groups?

Many church organizations are known to say that they welcome everyone, but do they truly? At a large national conference of a Catholic professional group, hospitality seemed to be the main agenda for the newcomers who were coming to the convention for the very first time. They were given different-colored nametags so they could be easily recognized; they were invited to a special welcoming luncheon; they were invited to a special reception for newcomers on the night of the banquet. They were impressed with the lengths to which this national organization went to welcome them as newcomers.

Upon attending a few of the events, however, the newcomers soon found out that while hospitality was on the institutional agenda, it was not on the agenda of the existing members. Attempts by the newcomers to introduce themselves were politely rebuffed; an overture made by a newcomer to join a group for lunch or dinner was discreetly discouraged. This was, in reality, an "old boys' club," and newcomers, men and women alike, were in actuality not welcome. Cliques had been formed. The old members showed they were not the least bit interested in welcoming the new members.

Similarly, authentic welcoming is not always communicated by official parish greeters. Occasionally, both greeters and ushers at masses welcome others insincerely; cynically, these may be called "robot-greeters." It almost appears that someone has wound them up with a key so they automatically shake hands and mumble, "Good morning." Or worse, they line up in a row and talk to each other, ignoring those coming in for mass. A remedy for this is to place the greeters themselves strategically both inside and outside of the church, away from one another. As someone approaches the church, they can step forward, extending a hand in greeting or a hug to a friend or neighbor. An identifying badge, nametag or sash is also helpful in making them more comfortable in their role of greeting people.

The whole purpose of the ministry of greeters is to welcome people as if they were long-lost friends, to let them know that not only are they happy to see them, but the whole parish rejoices that they have come. Perhaps this is a little overstated, but a greeter has the opportunity to welcome someone to mass much as a host or hostess welcomes guests to a dinner party. Just as the host or hostess is glad to see the person who has accepted the invitation and warmly welcomes the guest, attempting to make him or her as comfortable as possible, in the same way the greeter can engender the similar feelings of acceptance.

Beyond Greeters

Does the parish have a vibrant, practical, working welcoming plan that goes beyond providing greeters at church? Are the parishioners trained to welcome the stranger?

Once, when visiting a church for the first time in a strange city, a Catholic woman reported being surprised by the warm welcome she received, which began out in the parking lot. A couple came up to her and said, "Is this your first time here at St. X?" They introduced themselves and invited her to sit with them at mass, where they introduced her to a few other people. Everyone was so friendly!

It went even further. Instead of a general welcome to everyone at the beginning of mass, the pastor surprised her with a unique way of welcoming everyone and introducing visitors immediately after the petitions, when everyone was standing. The pastor asked everyone to remain standing and then asked only the members of the parish to sit down. This, of course, left the guests and visitors remaining standing so the pastor could recognize and introduce all of the guests to the rest of the parish. People sitting around the guests were then able to easily identify the visitors or newcomers, shake hands in welcome and hand them a "Welcome to Our Parish" handbook.

This handbook included a tear-out card at the front that gave many options to the guests. They could check off that they were just visiting the area or that they had recently moved into the neighborhood. They could ask for a personal appointment with a priest. They could give their address and phone number for a follow-up visit or to receive the monthly newsletter. The handbook included listings of the many ministries and services that the parish offered as well as the names and phone numbers of those in parish leadership. Every effort was made throughout this booklet to make them feel welcome.

After a lively and engaging mass, the couple from the parking lot invited the woman to stay for coffee and donuts in the parish hall, where they introduced her to the pastor, some of the staff and a few more parishioners. She was sorry that she didn't live in their community. "What a warm and welcoming parish," she thought to herself. "We should try this in my own parish!"

The most amazing part of this incident is that the woman discovered there was no welcoming committee; the entire membership of the church was the welcoming committee. This was an *evangelized* and an *evangelizing* faith community. The members were delighted to share their faith in God with others. Because they knew who they were—children of God— there was no competition, fear nor cliquishness. Neither threatened by the newcomers nor apathetic toward them, they simply welcomed them.

There is often a direct correlation between the demeanor of the greeters and ushers and the demeanor of the parish as a whole. Where the greeters and ushers are appropriately friendly, outgoing, welcoming and prayerful, the worshiping communities likewise are joyful, enthusiastic in their singing and responses, attentive to each other and hospitable. There is a sense of pride exhibited, which not only says, "Welcome to our parish!" but "This is the greatest parish in the world!"

The reverse also applies: Where the greeters and ushers appear distracted, unfriendly, rushed, authoritative, overly aggressive or preoccupied with tasks during the liturgy, the worshiping assembly quite often has a similar nature. Somberness and an impersonal quality are the hallmarks of these assemblies. The mass does not seem to be celebrated so much as endured.

Obviously, the question arises: Do joyful, friendly greeters and ushers create joyful, friendly parishes, or vice versa? We have, once again, the chicken-and-egg quandary. Fortunately, we don't have to decide which comes first. The point is that, in either case, both the greeters and ushers undoubtedly have the potential to affect the style and tone of worship by their attitude and demeanor from the first moment they greet the people.

Ushers—Unsung Heroes

Depending on the era and the needs of the faith community, the role of ushers has changed radically over the centuries. Deeply steeped in scripture and tradition, ushers historically have been called gatekeepers, doorkeepers, temple guards and porters. As early as the third century before Christ, the lesser order of the doorkeeper had been established in Jerusalem and is the progenitor of today's ushers. The main task of this guild of gatekeepers was guarding the threshold of the city gates, just as their fathers had guarded the encampment of the Lord in previous generations. Not only did the doorkeepers guard the temple in ancient times, they were responsible for the donations offered by the people as well. By the time Christ was born, the doorkeepers had developed into the temple guard, which one church historian describes as "a paramilitary corps of police at the service of the temple priesthood." Members of this order were the ones sent to arrest Jesus in the Garden of Gethsemane and later to guard the tomb. (See *The Ministry of Ushering*, by Rev. Gregory Smith, Liturgical Press.)

While laypeople, both men and women, have served as ushers in modern times, it was not until 1972 that Pope Paul VI formally abolished the minor order of porter, a vestige of the gatekeeper role, which seminarians received, and thereby declericalized the ministry of ushering.

Ushering, as we know it today, has come a long way from the ancient notion of guarding the temple doors, but one can imagine that in countries where contemporary Catholics are or were being persecuted, the usher might serve as a lookout to protect the congregation or help keep the illicit gathering from being discovered.

In the same vein, while the role of ushering has retained the functions of collecting and presenting the offerings of the people, one suspects that in earlier times it also included "guarding" the offering or, in contemporary terms, making sure the collection gets to the sacristy or the rectory safely. Whatever the case, while today's ushers perhaps provide a far less dramatic role than that of a "temple guard," their role is as important now as it was in the early days of the church.

The differences between ancient and modern porters are striking. No longer an order requiring full-time residence, today the ministry of ushering is performed by the laity on a part-time basis. Indeed, today, instead of keeping people out of the temple, ushers are called to invite them in. No longer keeping watch to protect the congregation during times of persecution, they instead keep an "eye out" for those who have come to God's house.

Significant, Necessary, Critical Roles

Ushers carry out significant and necessary roles during liturgical celebrations in our churches. Wearing many hats, they perform a variety of tasks during the liturgy. We can easily think about all of the obvious tasks and duties they have: greeting and seating people, collecting the offering, helping in the presentation of the offertory, assisting people during communion and distributing bulletins at the end (not at the beginning!) of mass. Not so obvious, however, are their preparatory tasks of adding additional seating if necessary, asking parishioners to present the gifts, directing traffic when the children or catechumens leave and return, keeping track of which pews are reserved, assisting the elderly or disabled, calling for help in an emergency and other tasks dictated by unpredictable happenstance. If all of our ushers "went on strike," do we realize how many duties would be left untended?

In spite of their importance, the ministry of ushering remains today one of the most ignored, misunderstood, unrecognized and unappreciated ministries. While their ministry is subtle and unobtrusive, as it should be, ushers are often overlooked as the liturgical ministers they truly are. In another important way, their ministry is often taken for granted and not understood—in their capacity to evangelize through the ministry of ushering.

A Person-Centered Ministry

All Christian ministries are centered around the person of Jesus Christ and are offered as loving service by the disciples of Jesus for the disciples (or future disciples) of Jesus.

Who are these disciples who serve Jesus in this person-to-person ministry of ushering? Men and women of all ages and from all walks of life conscientiously make a decision to serve Jesus and his church in the service of ushering. They choose to make a commitment to be present at a certain time at a certain place on a regular basis. This commitment, while it may not seem earth shattering, is not always easy to fulfill. It involves sacrifices made by the ushers and by their families. Like the rest of us, sometimes they would prefer to stay snuggled deep under the covers on a snowy Sunday morning or, in good weather, play an early-morning round of golf. They may be so overwhelmed with their own problems at work or at home, that it takes all their energy to show up on time.

In the same vein, ushers clearly reflect the range of moods that the members of the congregation feel. For any number of reasons, the last place some of the parishioners may want to be is at church. They might be sick, worried or just wish they were on the golf course. They might be returning to church for the first time in years, with all the associated fears.

They could be very angry with one of the parish staff or a member of the parish or even the church itself. Some may be experimenting with various expressions of faith and are attending mass for the first time out of sheer curiosity. Or maybe they have been dragged to church by their spouse, for the sake of the children.

The point—and it's a very important point—is that, whatever their dispositions, these people *are* present, both ushers and congregants. The ushers, however, have a special duty to be sensitive to the mood, the pain, the hurt, the illness, the "whatever" of those attending mass. This is all part of living out the paschal mystery, the dying and rising, which we all must experience in our lives. The sensitive usher, in his or her own unique way, walks with the other, offering a kind word, a gentle touch, an understanding glance, an important piece of information, a compassionate response, as the Spirit moves within, no matter how he or she may feel at the moment.

A Ministry of Presence

Ushers, in a particular way, exercise a ministry of presence that brings a sense of constancy and stability to those attending mass. The presence of the usher serving week in and week out, often at the same mass, in the same location within the church, offers a conspicuous model of commitment.

What is the personal impact of this ministry of presence? Ushers have the opportunity to meet and greet the regulars at the mass, thus establishing a sense of community, even in a business-as-usual climate. Catholics arguably are creatures of habit and many prefer to sit in approximately the same location each Sunday. Consequently, people who regularly attend the same mass welcome the familiar face, the smile, the handshake and the nod of recognition from "their" usher. In the routine, a personal network is built. Unlike some other parish ministers, ushers have a unique opportunity to meet and speak with people as they arrive.

One usher reported recently, "Even with communication and contact limited to the formalities of the mass, I discovered when I served as an usher in my own parish at the noon mass every Sunday, always taking the same station on the right hand aisle, a certain sense of community arose between the regular participants and myself. Some of these people I knew; others were total strangers to me." He continued, "Eventually, though, as time passed I introduced myself after mass to some of those whom I didn't know, and we became acquaintances, meeting weekly. The right-hand aisle was our link. Our presence became significant and served as a form of bonding. If someone came without their spouse, I would ask about it. Or if someone came up the aisle on crutches, I would inquire about the circumstances and assure them of my prayers during mass. If a family was not present for a few weeks, I might even call them to see if everything was okay. Once, when a regular widow did not come for three weeks in a row, I called her just to say that I missed her and wondered if she had been ill. She was so grateful for my call!"

Sometimes people feel that no one would even notice whether they came to mass or not, or that no one would notice whether they moved out of the neighborhood, or even left the church entirely, choosing to go to a church of a different denomination. This makes clear the importance of noticing the presence or absence of others in the community.

Hospitality

Of course, the "irregulars" may be attending mass also, approaching the usher's "territory" without the benefit of recognition. For the observant usher, this provides an even greater opportunity for practicing hospitality and welcoming the stranger. This is where the benefit of a weekly commitment by the usher is so valuable. An usher who has served regularly at a given mass can more easily identify the "stranger" and give an appropriate welcome.

Ushers complement and reinforce the ministry of the greeters or welcoming committee. After the person has been greeted at the door of the church, he or she moves inside and encounters the ushers. This encounter has the potential of being a very positive, welcoming moment—or a very negative experience if met by a pushy usher. Sincerity is the key to hospitality.

Welcoming is particularly important for the person who is arriving at the church for the first time. Not knowing anyone or not being familiar with the physical arrangements of the church can be quite threatening or stressful. What a welcome breath of fresh air it is to enter a church where someone goes out of their way to greet you, whether you are known or unknown. Ushers can relieve anxiety or uncertainty by assuring newcomers that, first of all, they are most welcome and, second, through the subtle communication of human exchange, ushers can implicitly say, "We are proud of who we are, and we want you to be a part of us!" This doesn't take much. A few words like: "Hi! Have I met you before? I'm so and so....Oh, this is the first time you've come here? Well, we are so glad you are here today! Can I help you find a seat? Have you met the Smiths yet?" People suddenly feel like they belong.

The Critical Role of the Usher

The usher's role can also be critical at times, entailing responses to emergencies and crises in the church. While high-tech electronic security systems, as well as local police departments, now provide most of the "guarding of the doors" of our churches, an alert usher often makes the difference in times of crisis. Our own experience in pulpits across the United States have provided us with many occasions where we have been most grateful for the ushers who have responded quickly and efficiently to serious emergencies in parishes we have visited.

Illness: During mass, an elderly woman became quite ill and appeared to be having a heart attack. Because of the watchful awareness of the ushers and their prearranged emergency planning, one usher called the paramedics immediately, a second usher quietly cleared the surrounding pews, a third offered CPR and a fourth comforted the family of the sick woman. As the woman was being wheeled out on a gurney, accompanied by both paramedics and ushers, prayers were said by the whole congregation for her. A great sense of peace and calm permeated the entire incident, with well-trained ushers knowing exactly what to do. Calm prevailed instead of chaos!

Intrusion: At another parish, during the middle of mass, a woman dressed in a long, flowing robe and carrying a ten-foot cross marched down the aisle. The elderly, retired celebrant who often helped out on the weekends actually thought that her appearance was planned by the parish staff as part of a presentation, a gimmick to get the people's attention to invite the parishioners to the parish picnic later that day. It wasn't planned at all! She began to spew satanic remarks directly at the priest. One panicked glance at the ushers brought them immediately to his rescue. Two ushers gently but firmly led the woman away from the altar. The priest apologized to the assembly for the interruption and continued mass, grateful for the swift response of the ushering team. Known by the police, whom another usher had called immediately, the woman was a mental-health patient who lived in the community and had frequently caused other disturbances.

Danger: Various occasions when there have been threats made against the presider or the whole assembly have necessitated emergency action from the ushers. In one case, ushers whisked a guest speaker out of the pulpit when they received an anonymous telephone threat against him. On another occasion there was a bomb threat, and the ushers responded by evacuating the entire church in an orderly and timely manner. A third example came when an usher noted that one of the parishioners attending mass had a gun strapped to his ankle. The police were called immediately.

Although these emergency situations are few and far between, when they do arise the ushers play a critical role. By having a calming effect on the people, they help diminish hysteria in a large crowd, which could be more damaging in the long run than the initial emergency. If ushers not only know what to do but have a sense of how to do it, they make a decisive difference by their presence in the congregation.

Ushers, then, like receptionists and greeters, put a human face onto our often anonymous-looking congregations. Even further, like other ministers, they put themselves aside for the sake of others, in the spirit of Jesus, and thereby help make him more visible to believer and seeker alike.

Reflecting on Our Ministry

• What is the tone set in my parish? Is it friendly, neutral or even cold?

• What is it like to call the rectory? How accessible do I feel the clergy or parish staff are to those who call?

• How busy and occupied is the reception space of the parish? Is it "stranger-friendly"?

• Does my parish have greeters at each mass? What is the effectiveness of this ministry? How open are greeters to newcomers and visitors to the church?

• What resources are made available for those who visit the parish?

• Do ushers and greeters hang around together or do they separate to greet parishioners and visitors at the various entrances of the parish?

• How are greeters and ushers respected in the parish community?

• Are greeters and ushers readily identifiable (e.g., by dress or nametag) by the congregation? What helps distinguish them?

• How able are ushers to recognize strangers?

• How well do ushers and greeters know the names of parishioners?

• How prepared are ushers for emergencies, questions or other unexpected incidents?

• How well is the collection of the parish made secure?

How can ushers help with this security? Are several people with the collection at all times?

• Can ushers and greeters readily refer people to the RCIA catechumenal process or the parish's ministry for inactive Catholics? What about inquiries made by youth, single parents, young marrieds, seniors or the recently bereaved?

CHAPTER FOUR

Eucharistic Ministers— Bringers of Christ

For my flesh is true food and my blood is true drink.
Those who eat my flesh and drink my blood
abide in me, and I in them.
John 6:55–56 NRSV

It is a thoroughly exciting liturgical moment. In the Cathedral in Cuernavaca, now stripped of its old baroque adornments and revealing the simple frescoes of the first encounters between European and native dwellers in sixteenth-century Mexico, the main mass features the preaching of the bishop and mariachi music. While both are memorable, the energy of the music lingers longer in the mind.

A sort of magnetism pulls every strata of the people of Cuernavaca together for this key celebration. One sees students and young adults, many tourists, established-looking families, prosperous businessmen, children and families from the simplest levels of Mexican life. They come in faith; they come for Christ. And they come to communicate in Christ.

One Sunday, a woman dressed very simply and without any pretense stood in the main aisle with her two-year-old in a stroller in front of her. Visitors noticed her standing and offered her their places in the pews. She smiled gratefully and refused. The music engaged both mother and child, as the trumpets and rhythms grabbed the whole congregation. At communion time the mother went forward, wheeling her child in front of her. She returned to her space, obviously still consuming the body of Christ.

Then, in a totally transparent and startling gesture, she put her fingers to her mouth, took some of the eucharist she had received and passed it into the mouth of her child. Both she and the child smiled with the exchange, as if electricity had passed between them and, instinctively, both of them were celebrating it.

Food for the World

When Pope Pius X inaugurated the practice of extending communion to children, he surely did not have in mind the simple gesture of the Cuernavacan woman. Indeed, he and a host of liturgists and catechists might justifiably rail at the untrained boldness of this woman who presumed to feed her child with part of her communion bread. The eucharist asks for recognition, for consciousness, for some sense of mature awareness and response. Our Catholic tradition reserves it for those who are old enough to know the meaning of the consecrated bread, which has become Christ's body, and the wine, which has become Christ's blood.

Yet, if the eucharist begs for recognition, it also begs to be shared. It is bread for the world; the sacrament will only reach its fullness when, in some way, all come to feed on this food of God, the body that was handed over for the salvation of all, the cup of blood that was shed "for all," as we say during mass.

In Luke's Gospel, after Christ is raised from the dead, he goes (as all the other Gospels concur) unrecognized by even his closest followers. Two of them, Cleopas and a companion, are seen leaving Jerusalem as soon as they can after the Sabbath observance. They are returning home in defeat and disappointment. Joined by a Stranger, one they do not recognize, they continue their conversation. The Stranger gently gets the two companions to include him in their discussion. They are talking about Christ, his rejection and death, the failure of his mission. The trip culminates in the evening, as the three stop for a meal. "Stay with us; join us," they say to the Stranger. He stays with them and, during the meal, takes bread, says the blessing, breaks it and gives it to them. This is the same gesture that Jesus employed throughout his earthly life and, in particular, the gesture Jesus used the night he was betrayed. In the breaking of the bread, Luke tells us, Jesus was recognized (Lk 24:13 ff.).

One breaks bread to share it. When we are not eating alone, the very gesture of breaking bread leads our hands to pass the bread to our dinner companions. No one breaks the bread and then puts all the pieces on his or her own plate. No one breaks the bread and then hides it. The bread, once broken, is passed to everyone at the table. So also with Christ. His breaking of bread shows who his bread is for: "For you and for all," in the words used in the consecration. It is bread, potentially, for the world.

Every minister of the eucharist, bishop, priest, deacon, eucharistic minister, acolyte or altar server has to personally feel the tension of the bread of Christ, the urge for that bread to be broken and shared. Since bread is a universal food, the staff of life, in one way or another throughout all human cultures, so the breaking of the bread and its sharing represent the dynamic intention of God to bring divine life to the whole world.

Our ministry of the bread and the cup, therefore, is an inherently evangelizing ministry. As the believers are fed, so the hearts of the believers are turned to all those who do not yet believe, to those away from the table, to those who still hunger for life.

Here arises the great paradox of the love of God: It is universal and unconditional, but it must be accepted and received. The waters of baptism are available to everyone, but who will descend into them? The bread of Christ is food for the world, but who will have the faith, the vision, to see what this bread means and eat it in faith?

Jesus went through the very same issue with his own disciples after they had witnessed, twice in Mark's account, his marvelous feeding of the hungry. "Do you not understand about the bread?" he chides them, after they miss his point about the "leaven of the Pharisees" (Mk 8: 14–21). Bread represents life, and eating the bread represents a way of life. God can feed, but eating the bread that God gives means living in a definite, trusting relationship with him and his community.

John's Gospel makes the same point, once again in connection with Jesus' feeding of the multitude. Those who have been fed continue to pursue Jesus to the point where he asks them: "Are you following me because you saw the sign or because you had your stomachs filled?" (Jn 6:26). The price of eating the bread of God is this: to believe in Jesus, whom God has sent (Jn 6:29).

The bread that God offers to feed the world, the food of Christ, demands faith. This is the sacramental mirror of the paradox of God's unconditional love: It must be accepted. The bread must be eaten in faith. Some of our modern sensitivities run counter to the demand for faith, and the eucharistic minister can feel particularly defensive. When the church puts limits on who can properly receive the eucharist, we can sometimes feel unfairly restricted. But unless the bread continues to demand faith, will it not eventually lose its meaning?

The Food of Faith

So what kind of faith is the eucharist asking of the believer? When the eucharist is broken, shared and distributed, what is the mystery in which the Christian is involved?

All of the scriptural narrations about feeding, from those of Moses in the desert, through the table fellowship of Jesus with his disciples and with sinners (e.g., Mt 9:9), through his feeding of the multitudes, through the eating Jesus did with his disciples after his resurrection (e.g., Jn 21:4–8; Lk 24:41), have been indelibly shaped by the food Jesus gave at the Last Supper. Gathered with his disciples the night before he died, Jesus reveals the stakes of what it means to eat with him.

Every act of sharing the eucharistic food of Christ simply extends in time the gesture of Christ gathered with his followers on that last occasion. Eucharistic ministers can do their ministry fully only if they continually advert to the meaning of eating Christ's bread and drinking from his cup.

Although scholars, reflecting on the varying accounts of the Last Supper, continue to debate whether it occurred during a Passover meal or not, the "paschal" character of the Last Supper cannot be evaded. Something dramatic is happening here; Jesus is "passing over," and "giving over," giving himself absolutely.

During the traditional Jewish blessings over the food—a custom that would have been strong among the pious Pharisees through the table fellowship that characterized their, and Jesus', way of life—Jesus adds to the blessing those words that have come to define his meal: "This is my body which is given for you," and, "This is the cup of my blood which will be shed for you and all for the forgiveness of sins." Making this gesture into an enduring ritual for his followers, he adds, "Do this in memory of me" (e.g., Lk 22:17–19; Mk 14:22–25; Mk 26:26–29).

Putting ourselves into this setting, the solemn moment of Jesus' passing over in love in response to the Father, what could this moment mean? As the disciples ate and drank, what could have been dawning on them? As the church continues to be in Christ's living memory by the repetition of this ritual feeding again and again throughout its entire history, what is the meal asking?

It is, in its plain and open meaning, an invitation to share in the passing over of Jesus himself. It is a partaking in him as he dies and rises. The bread that Christ gives is a share in his "broken" body. The cup that Christ passes is the cup of the blood that was "shed." To eat the bread and drink the cup is to accept Christ's death—and resurrection—as one's own. It is to die with him again, so as to experience his resurrected new life.

In the great Protestant revival tradition as practiced in modern times, there usually is a part of the service named "the altar call," when the preacher or minister asks anyone who wants to be saved to respond to the Word, to please come forward.

Every Catholic eucharist is an altar call. Every approach to receive the body and blood of Christ in communion is an invitation to gives one's life to God in the exact pattern of Jesus Christ, to die with him, because only through that death can we come to experience the new life that Jesus bestows through the Holy Spirit.

Of course, this means real Presence, as we Catholics describe the transformation of the bread into Christ's truly risen Body and the cup of wine into Christ's own life-giving blood. Yet, the real Presence itself demands a real response. It demands the giving of ourselves in faith to the dying and rising of Christ. It demands, in short, our ongoing conversion.

A Ministry of Evangelizing

Although much of Catholic experience in the last millennium betrays practices and patterns that "protect" the sacredness of the mystery of the eucharist through restriction and reservation, the church never saw the eucharist as anything other than bread for the world.

Even prior to the twentieth century, when reception of the eucharist was only an annual event for most Christians (both of the Western and Eastern churches), the eucharist was still the center of Catholic life, encased in a prominent tabernacle or enthroned in a gilded monstrance. However, the twentieth century, beginning with the papacy of Pius X, has been characterized by an opening of access to the eucharist. Pius X urged frequent communion as well as reception by children as soon as they could recognize the eucharistic mystery.

Under Popes Pius XI and Benedict XV, the beginnings of the renewed liturgy were explored. Popes Pius XII and John XXIII reduced the eucharistic fast to make it more possible for Catholics to receive. The eucharistic reforms of the Second Vatican Council turned the altar around and said, in effect, that the mass was a meal at which everyone present should eat.

Through much of the history of the Christian West, the eucharist was not reserved for those at the church service itself. It was carried beyond the Christian gathering to those who were sick. Even as early a writer as St. Justin Martyr in the second century A.D. talks about the "deacons" bringing the blessed bread to those who "were not present." Early church history describes the practice of Christians carrying the leftover eucharist home in little boxes called *arcae* for use at home during the week; Christians even kept the eucharitic bread on their persons in linen sacks for personal protection.

The recent expansion of the ministry of the eucharist through the Roman instruction *Immensae Caritatis* returns to some of these earlier customs in which the sacredness of the mystery was demonstrated not only by what we did in the church gathering but also by how the eucharist was brought to those who could not be part of the church assembly.

Today's role of the "extraordinary minister of the eucharist," or the "eucharistic minister" arises from this new instruction, responding to various pastoral needs that the renewed liturgy imposes upon us. Whereas once less than half the congregation would approach the altar to receive, today almost the entire congregation will come forth. Whereas rectories housed several priests for a concentrated Catholic population living in cities, today rectories house only one or two priests, and Catholics are scattered in numerous parishes throughout cities, suburbs and rural settings. Whereas receiving communion was usually done only under the form of the consecrated bread, today congregations celebrate the full sign of the eucharist by receiving both the consecrated bread and cup.

What, for a large part of recent history, then, was never seen, has become a common sight at virtually every Catholic church. In fact, when Catholics today do not see lay men and women and religious sisters and brothers participating in the distribution of the eucharist, it strikes them as strange.

With hundreds of eucharistic ministers commissioned in diocese after diocese, the implications of being a eucharistic minister—and the evangelizing implications of this ministry—cannot be ignored. The eucharistic minister helps in the distribution of the food of Christ, both to the assembled congregation and to those who, because of age or illness, cannot be present. As the distributor of the body of Christ, the eucharistic minister literally brings Christ to the world.

The suggested rite for commissioning a eucharistic minister puts the issue succinctly: "Are you resolved to undertake the office of giving the body and blood of the Lord to your brothers and sisters, and so serve to build up the church?" This is the question asked of the ministers. It shows the point of their ministry: to build up the church, to make Christ's community truly his body, to participate in that gathering of all humankind in the Holy Spirit, in the family of faith.

The Human Element

While the responsibilities of eucharist ministers vary from parish to parish and from diocese to diocese, there are several factors common to most situations that occasion reflection on this ministry.

Eucharistic ministers help bring about the powerful moment when a believer is sacramentally united with the Lord. How the ministers conduct themselves within the whole liturgy can make these moments either an empty routine or a deep experience of Christ's presence. How the eucharist is distributed, both in the church and in the homes of those who cannot attend mass, directly affects how readily Christ's presence is felt and responded to.

How do we attend to the people who come forth for communion? Do we even see them in this intimate religious moment, or is it simply just one person after the other? In our own communicating and in the communicating of the other faithful, are we, as eucharistic ministers, unambiguously aware of the union Christ is bringing about?

There are certain points eucharistic ministers can reflect on to help attune them to the deeper evangelizing dimension of their ministry:

1. *Attitude:* Immediately before we begin to serve eucharist to others in the assembly, we have all agreed with the presider's statement, "Happy are we who are about to receive." Does our attitude in service reflect "happiness"? Do we joyfully serve the consecrated food, or do we seem noncommittal? As we offer the host to our brothers and sisters, do the words, "The body of Christ," become a rote phrase? As we say, "The blood of Christ," do we offer the cup to

others with peaceful joy? Do we, by the way we conduct our ministry, say yes to their faith?

One parish member often complained that either the priests or the eucharistic ministers often served communion almost on an assembly-line basis: "Body of Christ...Body of Christ...Body of Christ...," repeated in monotone, with no recognition of the individuals receiving. Does not our whole attitude change as we recognize the relationship and honor the individual? We can recognize distinct feelings when we serve communion to our spouse or children or best friend. Do we have analogous feelings toward others? Do we feel a tremendous bond between each other, a bond that goes far beyond the ordinary?

2. *Empathy:* As eucharistic ministers, are we aware of the needs and concerns of the people whom we serve? Does our eucharistic mission take on a special meaning as we serve a crippled, elderly woman assisted up the aisle by her equally crippled husband? How do we feel when we have the privilege of serving a mentally impaired youth, a paraplegic, or a teenager with Down's syndrome? Do we notice the tears in the young mother's eyes or the acceptance in the widower's expression? Are we aware of the spiritual hunger of the teenagers we serve? The empathy we feel in these situations reflects, through the human interchange, the union of the believer with Christ, whose broken body took on all human struggle and striving.

Our service as eucharistic ministers need not end with the final blessing or recessional hymn. With our public role, we also have a kind of permission to approach others precisely because we are recognized. Can we not seek out and comfort the young tearful mother? Can we not find the elderly couple or the physically afflicted and offer them encouragement on their journeys? When the priest is being crowded after mass by scores of parishioners, that might be an opportunity to approach someone we have noticed with reassurance, a helping hand, a word of advice or even a simple smile.

3. *Presence:* As eucharistic ministers, we are usually assigned regular schedules whether they are daily, weekly or monthly. The more frequently we serve, the more opportunities arise for becoming acquainted with other parishioners, especially when we serve at the same station on a regular basis, like ushers and other regular ministers at mass.

Often, communicants will blurt out to a eucharistic minister comments that they feel would needlessly take up the priest's time after mass. Simply by virtue of the trust implied in their ministry, eucharistic ministers are viewed as worthy of their confidence. Eucharistic ministers report comments ranging from "My arthritis is acting up again, please pray for me," to "I am so worried about my teenage daughter," or "If only John would find a job soon!" Because we are sacred ministers, it is always appropriate to offer prayer for these people and, as appropriate, to offer real physical or emotional support, such as in the case of a needy family or an elderly widow. Also, if a communicant describes or you observe a truly serious situation, it is critical that you report it to the pastor as well as offer resources for immediate referral to appropriate social agencies or medical services.

The key to all of this is the physical and emotional presence of the eucharistic minister, not only during the mass but beyond it as well. Communicants already feel a bond with the one who has served them communion and are far less hesitant to speak to someone they "know" rather than to a total stranger. It is up to the eucharistic minister, however, to provide the time, the space and an inviting and welcoming presence.

4. *Involvement:* Many eucharistic ministers value highly the opportunity to serve communion to the homebound and believe that their service is most rewarding when they are additionally involved in the family's or communicant's life. Even so, it is sometimes tempting, when one has many communion calls, just to zip in and out quickly. Some eucharistic ministers, especially those who are unemployed or who have retired, have all the time in the world for their ministry; others simply do not have enough time for adequate visits and should consider limiting their visits to homebound communicants to one or two a week. In either case, though, after serving communion in the prescribed manner and allowing the communicant adequate time for reflection and thanksgiving, the eucharistic minister should not rush out immediately. He or she should at least offer the communicants the opportunity to personally share further if they so desire. With many of the sick and homebound, eucharistic ministers can develop deep and lasting friendships. The minister who brings communion to the sick also has the responsibility to link them with the resources, both personal and parish, that they need.

The eucharistic minister, when bringing the eucharist to the sick, becomes part of the healing dimension of the sick person's life. The eucharist itself heals through the presence of Christ and the consolation Christ brings. If the illness involved is terminal, the eucharist brings acceptance and peace. If it is a curable, treatable, but long-term illness, such as therapy for a stroke victim, the eucharist brings courage. The attitude of the eucharistic minister is paramount in cases such as these.

The eucharistic minister, as an evangelizing minister, has a myriad of opportunities to reflect the six dimensions of evangelization, especially to the homebound: discipleship, friendship, witness, proclamation, invitation and integration into the community. The evangelizing minister becomes one of the main links between the sick or elderly person and the parish community. Evangelizing eucharistic ministers, aside from offering genuine friendship and support as disciples, have the unique opportunity to witness their faith through their committed service, to proclaim the Gospel with the communicants through the reading of scripture and the mutual sharing of faith stories, to invite the communicants into a deeper relationship with Jesus and to integrate them into the parish faith community by bringing them news about the parish and the neighborhood. The eucharistic minister can also invite the homebound to be involved in appropriate ministries, such as being members of a telephone prayer chain.

5. *Serving:* Obviously, eucharistic ministry is not about building up ourselves. While the ministry, with respect for the people of God, demands a care about one's preparation, spirituality, awareness, empathy, compassion and even physical appearance when one comes to serve, the ministry is hardly about our "looking good" and making a great presentation of ourselves. Even priests, if they will ever be effective ministers, come to realize that church is not about them and how well they are doing. In recruiting and training people for eucharistic ministry, both the parish and the individual Catholic have to exercise great discernment so that the ministry will be motivated by service, by a generous desire to build up the body of Christ, to

bring Christ to the world so that the world may be transformed through saving faith.

6. *Inviting:* All those involved in the ministry of the eucharist bear the special responsibility of extending its evangelizing dimensions beyond the actual sacramental moment. As one who feeds in the name of Christ, the minister can be specially sensitized to those who hunger for faith. Who else can more convincingly invite others to experience Catholic worship than those who perform the extraordinary ministry of helping to distribute the Lord's food? The pride that every practicing Catholic has in his or her parish should be all the greater in those who serve the parish in such a public and sacred way by their eucharistic ministry.

Evangelizing Actions and the Eucharist

By reflecting on certain dimensions of the eucharist, we can begin to see the range of actions that are part of a eucharistic way of life, a life based in the eucharistic reality of Jesus Christ in the church.

Eucharist is Word and Worship: The mass shows the dynamic and necessary connection between the Word of God and the whole liturgy. Just as Jesus enlightened the disciples on the way to Emmaus with his words and then revealed himself in the breaking of the bread, so we cannot fully partake in the bread without also opening up the meaning of God's Word. This happens not only for the personal spiritual life of every eucharistic minister, extraordinary and nonextraordinary; it also has to happen for every person who is to be fed with the eucharistic bread of Christ. *The way we attend to and proclaim the word, whether it's on the altar or in the bedroom of someone who is sick or in daily life, enables us to begin to access the full meaning of Christ's eucharist.*

Eucharist is table meal: Jesus gathered his followers and those who needed him around his table as a regular part of his ministry. In the mass we see this table ministry made present in our own day. However else we are called to think about the eucharist, it is clearly a gathering around the table. It is a ritual meal. Therefore it has to have some of the same human and spiritual gestures of a meal. The gathering of everyone around the table, their sense of being invited and being welcomed, their sense of participation in the action, all are essential components of making it possible for people to be around the table of Christ. *As ministers of the eucharist, we have to insure that invitation and welcome characterize our Catholic way of life–not only at the mass itself, but in our attitudes toward all people. These initial relationships make it possible for people to someday think of themselves as included in our table fellowship.*

Eucharist is food for the journey: The earliest images of the eucharist compared it to the "manna" that God poured down upon the Jewish people in the desert—the peculiar food that accompanied them during their long road through the desert prior to entering the promised land (see Ex 16:13 ff.). As Christians understand themselves as pilgrims and wayfarers, so the image of eucharist as food for the journey, the bread without which we cannot survive, takes on great importance. Eucharistic ministry to the sick powerfully demonstrates the ongoing connections between all of us pilgrims and the way the burdens of illness are carried by all. Our reflections on the strengthening bread of the wayfarers should not, however, be limited to just those who are ill and elderly. *The eucharist calls all of us to an ongoing sense of pilgrimage and a resistance to any illusion that the fullness of the kingdom is "here" in our present experience.*

Eucharist is the gift of Christ: Eucharistic ministers in particular have to live in *eucharist*—in "thanksgiving" for the gift of Jesus Christ, eternally given by the God of love, and given again and again in the sacramental interchange of the liturgy. Our Catholic belief in the real Presence calls us to continue to stretch the ways we acknowledge, without falling into superstition or theologically naive thinking, that Christ is truly present in the eucharist. This awareness of the true presence of Christ as gift to us makes us "Christ bearers" to the world, for Christ's presence does not cease when the eucharistic food is consumed. *How we reflect Christ's ongoing gift to the world has to transform our whole approach to this ministry.*

Eucharist is the gift of self to God in Christ: Eucharist is not only Christ's gift of himself; in Christ, we give ourselves in turn in obedient love to God through the Holy Spirit. In this way, we are one with the eucharist as *sacrifice*—as loving gift of ourselves in Christ who, through dying and rising, gives himself in love as saving sacrifice for the world. *Just as we, every time we receive, are called to give ourselves again radically and totally to God in Christ, so when we administer the eucharist to others we partake in the call to them to give their lives in sacrificial gift to Christ.*

Eucharist is union: The Gospel of John draws out so clearly the unifying dimension of the eucharist: "Those who eat my flesh and drink my blood, abide in me and I in them" (Jn 6:56). St. Paul also emphasizes the "one bread and the one cup" that has to bring unity to the "one body" of the church that feeds upon it (1 Cor 10;17; see also 1 Cor 11:17 ff.). Partaking in the eucharist, then, demands that we be in union with God and in union with each other; if not, the gesture is saying one thing while our lives are saying something else. *Eucharistic ministers further evangelization by making their union with God and with others a dominant framework of their own spiritual lives. Working for that union—and resisting anything that would diminish it—puts a particular burden on those who distribute the body of Christ.*

Eucharist is challenge: Eucharist demands that all those who partake of it live for a new world, a world of union with God and each other, a world of peace and wholeness, a world that responds to the kingdom that Jesus proclaimed. No eucharistic minister can be content with the way things are, either in the church or in the world. We are called not to be seduced by the status quo of our present experience. *The eucharist always calls us to do more, to strive for the relationships that the meal of Christ is trying to reveal, particularly those based on the love of God for everyone and the inherent dignity that every person has in Christ.*

Eucharist is mission: We call the eucharist "the mass" from words of the Latin dismissal rite, *Ite Missa Est*, which mean "Go, the congregation is sent forth." In other words the eucharist commissions us for mission. The Word that is celebrated, the food that is eaten, the actions of worship and fellowship that constitute the mass all point beyond themselves to the way Christians need to be in the world. Perhaps the principal reason why the world is not evangelized now is that the mission, the "com-mission" aspect, of the mass has been muted. *Our response to the dismissal, "Thanks be to God," anticipates that great day when the universe itself will echo "Thanks!" to the all-loving God who transforms us with the salvation of Christ.*

Eucharist is adoration: One way or another, the eucharist has been reserved and preserved throughout the history of the church for two purposes: to bring the sacrament to those who could not be present with us and to call us to further worship through adoration. While the eucharist is primarily action—especially the action we perform together at mass—the meaning of this action, all the aspects of the eucharist we have been reflecting on here, cannot be appropriated by the believer without time for quiet reflection and adoration. No more than the meaning of the Word can be absorbed just by hearing it, can the meaning of the eucharist be apprehended just by eating it. Evangelization is hardly all "hoopla" and "hallelujah"—it also includes, particularly in our Catholic tradition, the reflective embrace of adoration. It is no wonder that the first followers of Jesus reached their greatest insights into Christ while they were adoring him—even if they still remained puzzled—as the scriptures tell us (e.g., Mt 14:33; 28:9; 28:17; Lk 24:52; Jn 9:38). *Through adoration, the evangelized eucharistic minister makes Christ the center of his or her life.*

Reflecting on Our Ministry

• Being a eucharistic minister means, to use a phrase of St. Paul, "respecting [or discerning] the body" (1 Cor 11:29) in all its senses: the body of Christ; the body of the church; our own bodies, which become temples and instruments of God's service through our ministry; and the body of the world, which cries out for redemption (e.g., Rom 8:22). How have I grown in respect during my service as a eucharistic minister?

• How do I dress when I serve as eucharistic minister? Do I arrive early enough and help prepare for the liturgy?

• Have I reflected on the scripture readings of the day and made God's word central in my own heart?

• How comfortable am I with the sick? How understanding am I of their limitations and difficulties? How much time do I spend with the sick? Do I connect them with the wider resources they need?

• After I take hosts from the church in the pyx, how reverent am I of the eucharistic presence?

• How personally involved am I with the congregation, and how do I reflect that involvement during and beyond my ministry?

• How personally self-conscious am I in ministering? Am I able to set my own ego aside in order to build up the body of Christ, the parish?

• Do I see my ministry extended beyond the distributing of communion, to parishioners and to those searching for Christ?

• Do I quietly and regularly reflect on the meaning of the eucharist?

CHAPTER FIVE

Lectors: Proclaiming the Good News

For as the rain and snow come down...
my word shall not return to me empty.
Isaiah 55:11 NRSV

The utter darkness of the parish church is broken only by the flickering of one large candle and hundreds of small tapers. The aroma of incense still tinges the air. In a solemn voice, the church has proclaimed that this, the vigil of Easter, is the most holy night of all because God has chosen this night to save us.

Still in subdued light, the lector approaches the pulpit. The celebrant has just proclaimed the start of the vigil, today's vestige of the ancient practice of staying up all night to read the sacred scriptures. The congregation has taken their seats and, in a silence so strong it shouts, the reading begins.

It's from Genesis, the opening chapter, one of the two stories of the creation of the world with which the Bible begins. "A reading from the book of Genesis..."—the words pierce the stillness. The vigil has begun. The proclamation of the Good News has commenced. The power of revelation is felt once again by the people of God.

Even if we have not ministered personally by reading at the Easter Vigil, we all have realized, over the decades since the Second Vatican Council, the power of God's Word. Lectors, who have been designated by the church to proclaim the scriptures, feel that power in a variety of particular ways—sometimes even by their nervousness.

Perhaps every lector remembers "the butterflies" when he or she first began to read. After the opening prayer, the lector approached the ambo with something less than full confidence, turned to the properly marked page, adjusted the microphone, cleared the throat several times and finally took a deep breath. "A reading from...," the lector began, maybe swallowing, licking lips in nervousness and pushing aside stage fright.

But somehow the power of the word took over. Somehow the knees stopped trembling, the butterflies disappeared and the Word of the Lord boomed forth with confidence and energy. The lector, through his or her own initial insecurities, uncovered the energy by which God's Word has sustained people for almost four millennia.

It's what Jeremiah discovered through his call to be a prophet. He was hesitant, unsure, untested, unwilling, but that Word came to him with the same power with which, through our lectors and preachers, it still comes to us.

> "...I am a man of unclean lips, living among a people of unclean lips; yet my eyes have seen the King, the Lord of Hosts!" Then one of the seraphim flew to me,

holding an ember which he had taken with tongs from the altar. He touched my mouth with it. "See," he said, "now that this has touched your lips, your wickedness is removed, your sin purged." Then I heard the voice of the Lord saying, "Whom shall I send?..." "Here I am," I said; "send me!"

Isaiah 6:5–8 NAB

Since, statistically, the fear of speaking before a group of people is second only to the fear of flying, it is not uncommon for a lector to be utterly terrified the first time at the ambo. With time, though, this fear passes, and the lector will be much more at ease. Each time a lector or commentator proclaims at liturgy, the task becomes easier as the comfort level behind the ambo rises and the level of confidence increases.

Why? Not merely because we have become humanly accustomed to reading. It is because of the power of the Word of God, its ability to shape us through the working of the Holy Spirit.

The Power of the Word

Like all the other ministers of the church, lectors can gain a lot of insight into who they are called to be by taking the time to examine the service they perform. Walking in procession, holding the lectionary aloft, stepping up to the ambo, proclaiming the word aloud, pausing in silent reflection and then, at the end of mass, exiting with the book held high once again, with the congregation following—the procession and the solemnity accorded the reading of the Word of God are the community's way of echoing what God's Word brings about in the church's life.

This procession and the gestures associated with the proclamation of the Word show the importance that the public proclamation of the holy scriptures has in the life of the church. When the Gospels are read by priest or deacon, the gestures can be even more elaborate, through the signing of the body with crosses on the forehead, lips and heart, the congregation standing up alert to the Word, incense offered and even the singing of the gospel words themselves. But every reading of God's Word has its solemnity.

With all these gestures, the church clearly says one thing: The public proclamation of the Word before the assembled congregation, in and of itself, enjoys an undeniable importance. Why?

In these days of almost universal literacy, why not just flash the references for the scripture passages on the wall and let people bring their favorite versions and translations? They could sit in the pews quietly, reading at their own pace, undisturbed by the pace or accent of the lector.

The church, however, does not do this. Understanding why we always proclaim the Word of God aloud can open up for the lector our Catholic belief regarding the power of God's Word to act on our lives.

Particularly in our modern era, we think of words as private events that occur somewhere between our ears. Words are for us to unravel, juxtapose or even muse about. Our modern literate world equips us to control words: to write words with pencil, ink or electrons, to transmit words at enormous rates in communications with others, to edit and delete words at will—our modern world tells us that we are masters of our words.

We have professions that dedicate themselves to words, some to such an extent that one can barely use those words unless one belongs to that profession. Lawyers, for example, speak their own language. Doctors have their ways of communicating and, scribbling on prescription pads, direct words in their own particular way. Radio announcers and television newscasters manipulate words with great dexterity. We pick up our remote controls and mute the words we don't want to hear or, hearing them, have them appear written on the screen as well, even in another language.

All this activity leads to a stream of words endlessly pouring through our minds, creating a private world shaped by the combination of words we choose to use, amplify and hear. We control words; we take them into our world, believing we are their masters.

God's Word, however, is not like that. God's Word is the sacred expression of God's inner self, revealed as the heart of what is absolutely real. God's inner being becomes Word in Jesus Christ; "the Word became flesh," as we recite it every Sunday, because we believe that God's love is so compelling and so generous that it spills out in the very sharing of God's own self through Jesus and the Holy Spirit.

It is God's Word, then, that comes to us. We do not control it, own it, manipulate it or decide to rearrange it. It comes to us as the expression of God—the mystery that reveals and conceals at the same time—that saves us. For centuries the Jewish people preserved God's Word, first in spoken form (traditions, songs, memories and aspirations) and finally as the Jewish scriptures that still claim us today. For more than a century the first Christians, remembering Christ and reflecting on their lives through the Jewish scriptures, first spoke and then wrote down what we call the New Testament.

This whole process of speaking and writing, with all its communal influences over the centuries, came about through the process we call inspiration, under the influence of the Holy Spirit of God.

God's Word comes to us; it shapes us. It calls and challenges us. It forms us into God's people. It makes us who we are.

God's Word, in whatever mysterious ways it arose among the Jewish people and the earliest Christians, was never meant only for private consumption. It arose in the midst of God's people, in the community that God was bringing about, through the community's language and experience. It was meant to be proclaimed aloud in community and to be interpreted by community. God's revelation—and redemption—does not come first to *me*; first it comes as God's gift to *us*, making us God's people.

Similarly, the meaning of the Word is not on the page, nor in the movement of lips or even in the vibration of eardrums. The meaning is in the hearing, as the Word comes alive, interpreted again and again in and through the experience of the individuals and the community that hears it. This certainly does not mean that every community can decide what God's Word means. Rather, every community, standing under God's Word and being shaped by it, makes it a living Word as it hears and obeys that Word in the reality of its own experience.

This is our Catholic understanding of how God continues to act upon us in the Word. The Word is an intrinsic dimension of evangelization. When reading, the lector enters this sacred passing on of God's Word, helping to make it a living and a saving Word in our contemporary lives. Through the lector, God's Word continues to shape the community of believers.

An Evangelizing Ministry

The ministry of lectoring, therefore, offers one of the most explicit opportunities for Catholic laypeople to literally announce the Good News of Jesus Christ. The sacred words of God's own Word come through the lips of the lector at mass. How essential, then, that our churches in this age of information and communication cry out today more than ever for lectors who are formed and informed, particularly in terms of the power of evangelization in their ministry.

By definition, it would appear that lectoring is already an evangelizing ministry just by virtue of the content of the readings proclaimed during mass. Some people may wonder, "If reading scripture out loud during mass, sometimes to hundreds of people at a time, is not evangelization, then what is?" So why are not all lectors, by their very ministry, seen as evangelizers?

To this valid question, the answer is: "Well, there's reading...and there's reading...." As anyone who has grown in the ministry of lectoring can attest, there's much more to lectoring than just standing in the pulpit reading the text in front of you.

Lectoring obviously includes one of the essential dimensions of the process of evangelization, that of public, verbal proclamation (although we shall see various shades of meaning in the word *proclamation*). Lectoring appears to automatically embody what Pope Paul VI very clearly and forcefully stated: "If the name, the mystery, the teachings, the life, the death, and the resurrection of Jesus of Nazareth are not proclaimed, there is no true evangelization" (*Evangelii Nuntiandi*, #21). But proclaiming the words and living the reality that gives meaning and credibility to the words are two different things. The verbal proclamation of lectoring is pretty sterile unless it is charged by the dynamic dimensions of evangelization. Proclamation remains just the movement of lips unless it includes discipleship, witness, invitation, care for others and humility before the Word of God.

The Lector as Disciple

The first of these essential elements is discipleship, and this goes to the very heart of the lector personally. If the lector has not experienced heartfelt conversion to Jesus Christ on a personal level, it will be impossible for him or her to proclaim the Word of God as effectively, with as much conviction and power, as God calls us to. Any literate person can stand before a group of people and read from the lectionary with dramatic inflections and perfect diction—those skilled in acting might put most of us to shame—but the words will not be heard, assimilated or believed as well as they would be if they had been read, even somewhat poorly or haltingly, by a believer.

Without in any way downplaying competence and the need to proclaim strongly, clearly and compellingly, the single necessary requirement for proclaiming the scriptures is faith. It is, after all, with faith that we read and hear the scriptures. It is faith that opens our hearts to the "two-edged sword" of God's Word that cuts through hypocrisy and allows the meaning of God's expression to penetrate to our very core. It is faith that lets us stand under the judgment of God's Word. The lector reads from that core of faith. God uses the lector to help the Word penetrate to the center of life, opening up God's revelation.

Perhaps we are unsure that this is really so. Don't we believe that there is power in the Word itself, regardless of who proclaims it? Yes and no. For example, is it not a tactic of some groups to quote scripture to others to try to sabotage their belief? Even nonbelievers can quote scripture in such a way as to make it nonsense, in a spirit of ridicule. Saying the words themselves obviously does not contain any magic. When used in destructive ways, scripture remains only words formed by human vocal chords or by ink on a page. It does not have the power of God.

To be an evangelizing lector and to read the scripture with effectiveness, discipleship is absolutely necessary because only by living the Word, attending to it with the same excitement, curiosity, puzzlement and joy that we read about in the lives of those who followed Jesus—only by living the Word does that Word *become* a living word, a word that leads to life. Of everything that discipleship can mean, most of all it means attending to the Word of God with the passion of an eager learner.

One of the most ancient practices in the church is *lectio divina*—meditative, prayerful dwelling on the Word of God. For many Catholics this is a personal devotion, as they read the Sunday or daily lectionary readings in the spirit of humble prayer, slowly pausing over each word to grasp the inferences and catch the scripture's subtle hints. The disciple leaves room in his or her life for the Word of God to shape life.

For the lector, this kind of meditative reading is an indispensable way to prepare to ascend the ambo and proclaim God's Word because it is a reading done not by playing with words but attending to the Word in faith.

Proclamation—"Scriptural Storytelling"

The lector who sees the evangelizing potential of the ministry can make a great difference in the parish faith community by being as prepared as possible. As we noted, real lectoring requires faith. But faith alone does not make for effective lectoring. Rather, faith, the basis of discipleship, gives rise to a whole discipline of presentation that can make the Word of God vibrant in a parish. Our belief and love for the Word as disciples lead us to serve its proclamation with all our skills.

Every lector has to spend real time preparing him- or herself to proclaim God's Word. Unfortunately after a while, even the best lectors can take this preparation for granted. What kinds of discipline and preparation might the lector do to get in touch with the evangelizing power of the Word—its witness, its invitation, its challenge, its ability to touch the deepest parts of the heart?

We might look at one example of preparation as a way to insure our own readiness to read the scriptures aloud. At one parish each lector is trained to proclaim the Word of the Lord from memory every Sunday. Without suggesting that we burn our lectionaries because our memories work so well, we might look at this form of preparation to see what it can tell us about preparation. It is called scriptural storytelling.

Scriptural storytelling actually goes beyond mere memorization or the more normal exegetical approach to training. How does it work? Each reading, first of all, is divided into three parts—beginning, middle and end. If a section is too long, it is further divided into three subsections. Depending on the length of the reading, these may be divided again until there is a specific number of sections and subsections, which the lector masters one by one.

The mastery of each section requires not only exegesis of the passage but a use of the imagination as well. The lector visualizes the words used, as well as the content and context of the passage. As the lector masters the reading, eventually all the words of all the sections will be memorized, but they will also be told as a complete story by visualizing the words through imagery, dialogue or characterization.

For example, the reading designated for Monday of Holy Week (Is 42:1–7) would be prepared, first, by reading the entire text silently and studying the appropriate commentary. Then it would be divided as follows:

1–4:   Description of Isaiah (characterization)
5:     Description of God (characterization)
6–7:   What God says to you (dialogue)

Notice how the application of imagery and dialogue helps the scriptures come through. We might look in detail at part I to provide an example:

Part I
Verses 1–4: Description of Isaiah
Verse 1
Exegesis: 1. *Servant* can be identified as historical Israel, ideal Israel, an Old Testament historical character living before or during the lifetime of the prophet, or the prophet himself. Choose one to imagine; for our purposes, we will choose the prophet himself.
Imagery: 1. *Here is my servant whom I uphold* (imagine God holding Isaiah upright in his hand);

my chosen one with whom I am pleased (imagine God's finger pointing at Isaiah and God smiling);
Upon whom I have put my spirit (think of a dove over Isaiah's head);
he shall bring forth justice to the nations (visualize Isaiah holding a scale of justice over a map).

Verse 2
2. *Not crying out* (imagine Isaiah not crying like a baby) *not shouting* (nor shouting from a bandbox);
not making his voice heard in the street (nor like a newsboy standing in the middle of the street vending his wares).

Verse 3
Exegesis: 3. A reference to God's mercy.
Imagery: 3. *A bruised reed he shall not break* (imagine a black and blue hollow reed—or a clarinet, if you prefer); *and a smoldering wick he shall not quench* (and a candle that is nearly burned out with a pitcher of water standing next to it on a table).

Verse 4
Exegesis: 4. *Coastlands*: the lands of the Mediterranean. In the Old Testament the word often refers to the pagan lands of the west.
Imagery: 4. *Until he establishes justice on the earth* (envision "Lady Justice" standing on a globe);
the coastlands will wait for his teaching (Imagine the Carolina or California coastlands waiting to enter a schoolhouse!).

Obviously, this method requires much more time than the ordinary preparation for lectoring, but the effects are far-reaching and long-lasting. The method allows the lector to absorb the entire reading into his or her own spirit; the extensive preparation shows in the reading.

Being a "proclaimer" of the Word asks that we take what the Word has engendered inside ourselves and project it in an appropriate way to the congregation. There is, then, an "inside" and "outside" to this dimension of being an evangelizing lector. Neither can be neglected if the ministry is to be effective. It would be hard to conceive of a keener image of learning as an intrinsic dimension of discipleship in Christ.

The Welcoming Lector

A second vital dimension of effective evangelization is hospitality. By the very public and prominent place the lector has at worship, he or she has many opportunities to be hospitable. Not only can the lector welcome members of the parish to the weekend liturgy, but he or she has many opportunities to welcome visitors and nonbelievers to the parish as well.

In some parishes, for instance, it is the duty of the lector to welcome everyone before mass starts. Some lectors not only give a general greeting to all, but use the occasion to ask if there are any visitors who may be appropriately introduced and greeted. They may also take this opportunity to introduce a new family who will be bringing the gifts to the altar during mass: "This morning, John and Mary Johnson and their three children, Katie, John and Kevin, will present the gifts. They have recently moved into our parish from Los Angeles."

But even if the parish does not have the lectors explicitly perform welcoming functions, the demeanor and style with which the lector proclaims God's Word helps establish the ambiance of the whole congregation. Anything the lector says, whether it is the reading, a prayer petition or a welcoming announcement, creates a verbal environment for the congregation. What if the lector's words lack enthusiasm and sincerity? A ho-hum welcome or announcement, for example, will not appeal to or engage the congregation—it tells people that their time and attention are not being respected. By the lector's demeanor, the congregation gets the feeling that it is being taken for granted.

Research in verbal communication reveals that facial expression has the strongest impact on the listener (relaying 55 percent of the real meaning of the message), followed by tone of voice (38 percent) and finally by the actual words (7 percent). In other words, "You can spot a phony a mile away." If sincerity eradicates phoniness, dwelling deeply in God's Word makes us sincere.

The lector, then, can have a demonstrable effect on the assembly through posture, body language, dress, tone of voice and facial expression. A welcoming lector not only has prepared by practicing correct pronunciation, diction and phrasing, but will also be responsive to all of the people in the assembly, turning both to the left and the right, establishing eye contact when possible. This is part of the incarnational—flesh and blood—reality of the Catholic faith.

With a greater level of comfort and confidence, the lector will be able not only to proclaim the Word of the Lord but to project a welcoming, inviting and enthusiastic attitude that says to each person at mass, "You're important! You have the privilege of hearing God's own Word. We are really glad that you are here."

Practice What You Preach—Witnessing

Witnessing is another essential component of effective evangelization that lays a special burden on the lector. We use the word *witnessing* here to mean the silent witness of one's life (rather than the definition sometimes associated with the evangelical church where a *witness* is a conversion story.) The witness of the lectors' faith in everyday situations in their families, workplaces and community corroborates and adds credibility to the message that the lector proclaims publicly.

Have you ever seen or known a lector who appears haughty or proud because of his or her role in the liturgy? Or a lector who is less than honest in his/her business dealings, or abuses his/her spouse or children, or acts "holier than thou" when not behind the ambo? Unfortunately, we all know such people, and we all know how such behavior makes it difficult for the scriptures to be heard.

Invitation

One of the purposes of the readings during the liturgy is to prepare the heart and mind to enter into the mystery of eucharist. While the readings obviously are informative (this is what God says to us through the inspired writers), they are also invitational (See how much God loves us!). Scripture is God's priceless resource that nourishes our soul and prepares us to receive Christ in communion. This is perhaps the most subtle and most important invitational role that the lector performs in liturgy: The lector invites the congregation from the experience of the Word to the experience of the table.

The Jesus who is proclaimed in prophecy and Gospel, becomes the Jesus who, as sacred lover of the soul, gives himself as food to those who believe.

Do lectors realize how very important their role is in the Liturgy of the Word? As conduits through which God's Word is being conducted, they are the ones helping to make the connection between Word and eucharist. The eucharistic table is the ultimate focus of the Word. Evangelizing lectors help the assembly move from listening to the Word, to loving the Word, to living the Word.

Playing such a pivotal role in the magnetic attraction of the eucharist, the lector's life has to be permeated with Christ's magnetism. If the lector feels the pull in his own life, if the lector can humbly help the congregation feel the pull in their worship, then the lector is responsible for the invitation going beyond the walls of the church building. Is the lector satisfied when the Word is effectively proclaimed at worship or in a prayer service? A lector whose heart is set afire with evangelization knows that the Word is spoken for the world, that it cries out to be heard beyond the church walls, that its power can call everyone to the presence of God.

As ministers of the Word, lectors have particular advantages when it comes to inviting others. We are not referring to any "come-and-see-me" kind of bravado that would be very unseemly in a lector. Rather, we refer to the greater familiarity with God's Word that the lector develops after years of ministry. This facility, built up by hours of preparation and reading, is a powerful resource for the lector when discussing faith with others. Research shows that talking about faith is one of the preconditions to invitation. Many Catholics, when they get into conversations about religion, feel very inadequate, perhaps needlessly. But lectors have considerably less reason to feel inadequate. When issues arise, when questions are asked, when advice is sought, when others approach, the lector has a wealth of personal reflection from which to draw.

Upon being approached by another over a particular concern, the lector can easily begin speaking from personal conviction. "I've long thought about the question you are raising. Because I read the scriptures to my Catholic congregation, I've had the opportunity to see what light God's Word sheds on your concern. Can we talk about this further?" Such an overture can advance the relationship further, making specific invitations to a particular person quite appropriate and apt.

When lectors take discipleship seriously, living in the Word they proclaim, it leads them beyond the ritual of procession and proclaiming into the broader service of being like Jeremiah or Isaiah or Paul, of being a needed prophet for the world today.

Reflecting on Our Ministry

• Do I prayerfully prepare for my role by reflecting on the prayers and scripture used in the eucharistic celebration well before the liturgy?

• Do I view myself as a servant, being sensitive to and putting the needs of the assembly first?

• Do I see myself as an evangelizer, inviting the assembly into a deeper and richer relationship with God through their service?

• Do I proclaim the readings with all the understanding and passion that the holy Word demands?. Do I believe what I proclaim? Am I convincing?

• Do I wear proper attire when reading scriptures?

• Do I establish and maintain eye contact with the members of the assembly, helping to keep their eyes averted from the missalettes?

• Is my style of proclaiming warm and inviting?

• Do I speak clearly so that all can understand the spoken words?

• Do I attend properly to the placement of the microphone and the other practical details of my role? Do I arrive early enough to read over the announcements, the petitions and the names of the people who are sick or who have died, being sure to pronounce their names correctly? Do I know the parish's plan for recessing with the presider?

• Do I pray before the procession? After the recessional hymn?

CHAPTER SIX

Raising Joyful Praise: The Evangelizing Musician

> *[S]acred music is to be considered the more holy in proportion as it is more closely connected with the liturgical action whether it adds delight to prayer, fosters unity of minds, or confers greater solemnity on the sacred rites.*
> Second Vatican Council,
> Constitution on the Liturgy, #112

We enter the church, curious but alert. We've never been here before. We are watching for every signal about what kind of faith community worships at this parish. We notice the obvious things—how people enter church, whether there are greeters or attentive ushers, how the ministers are preparing for the mass.

None of that, however, stands out so much as when the first chord sounds and the music that starts the liturgy begins. When the congregation sends forth a full-throated verse, backed up by musical instruments, with the cantor evoking song from the people seemingly without effort, we have been caught up in something...in the spirit of the moment, in the worship, in the congregation, in the Gospel.

Few elements define a parish's spirit so much as the energy with which it raises joyful praise through music.

Traveling throughout the United States and Canada, giving parish missions or workshops on Catholic evangelization has given us entrée to literally hundreds of different parishes. One of the beauties of this experience is the constant of finding the same mass being celebrated everywhere. This constant of the mass allows the particular gifts and spirituality of parishes to shine forth when they gather on Sunday. Within this constant, one of the major variants that we find from parish to parish is the music ministry.

What a difference the ministry of music makes in the way a community celebrates eucharist! We offer some examples, none too far afield from general Catholic experience.

Example: An eighty-year-old organist, who has always been the choir director in her parish, dutifully plugs away at "Now Thank We All Our God," played at half-speed. A handful of equally aging parishioners, gathered in the choir loft high above the back of the church, drones out the refrain, "...with hearts and hands and voices." It is, indeed, a gift to God, this ministry that has gone on for so many years, but perhaps it is a gift that hides other gifts as well.

Example: The choir, robed in chartreuse, sways its way down the aisle in a rousing, hand-clapping version of "Joshua Fought the Battle of Jericho, Jericho, Jericho..." and takes its place near the altar, continuing to sway and clap as the celebrant approaches. The congregation is all astir. So many gifts are being shown and shared. Many in the congregation sing along, though a large number also just watch.

Example: After warming up, tuning their guitars and endlessly adjusting microphones and speakers, the long-haired leader of the contemporary music group ensemble begins a foot-stomping version of a song that one of them felt inspired to write last Saturday night. The musicians smile knowingly at each other as they fumble for the right rhythm. Meanwhile, the congregation stares ahead, waiting for mass to begin.

Example: After welcoming the assembly and teaching a new gospel alleluia, the cantor invites the assembly to join the choir in a gathering song and...everybody sings. The verses of the responsorial are hauntingly sung by a young boy with the assembly joining in on the response; the communion hymn, Marty Haugen's "We Remember..." is passionately presented and prayed with the choir and assembly taking respective parts; and the recessional, "How Great Thou Art," is reverently sung by all.

Though some of these cases may appear overstated, all of them actually exist in today's parishes. Most Catholics, who have gone through the vagaries of church music over recent decades with results that vary like the above examples, immediately know that music ministry makes a large difference in how the congregation assembles around the Lord's table.

With the renewal of the liturgy since Vatican II, many parishes have realized the importance of the music ministry. They have taken steps to improve this service in their liturgies. The difference between those parishes that have stayed on automatic pilot—unable or unwilling to search out and secure competent, talented, well-trained liturgical musicians—

and those who have recognized the essential part sacred music plays in liturgy is dramatically obvious.

The fourth example given above is from a parish that we are very familiar with. By looking at some of the components in the music ministry of this parish, we can analyze some of the reasons why the music ministry is so effective.

First of all, the music director holds a master's degree in liturgical music from The Catholic University in Washington, D.C. She is a competent person, trained to be a professional in the ministry of sacred music.

But more important than her competence, the vibrancy of the music ministry is primarily due to the evangelizing spirit the director brings to her ministry. Her ministry, as she articulates it, flows out of her sense of gratitude for "the great things God has done" in her own life. Having personally experienced God, she has "tasted and seen the goodness of the Lord"—and she wants to share that faith with others. With her contagious faith and her magnetic enthusiasm, her ministry both invites and incites participation. She seems to be saying, through her ministry in the congregation, "Why on earth wouldn't you all want to sing your praise to God this morning?"

Because this particular minister of music is very much in touch with her story of faith, she brings her own conversion experience to both the other music ministers and to the assembly. She has become an evangelizer. Her prayer, rooted in her obvious love of the Lord and of the parishioners, grounds her music and fills her with joy. Tellingly, she does not think music ministry is about entertainment or applause. "We are not here to entertain; we are here to encourage and assist you in worship," she constantly reminds the congregation, particularly when they are prone to break out in applause.

When the modern popes say repeatedly that evangelization is not merely about words, but about the witness of the lives of the believers, they put a challenge before every Catholic, including those whose music assists the worship of the congregation. Our example of a successful music ministry reveals that its effectiveness comes from faith coupled with competence.

Before we explore in detail how music, when competent and faith-filled, leads to evangelization, we might well look at why we have sacred music in the first place.

The Feeling Side

Why do we have music at our worship? And why has it come to play such an important part in contemporary parish experience? After all, it's pretty easy to conceive of worship, particularly the Catholic mass, without any music at all. Indeed, do not many people trudge out of their beds very early on Sunday morning so they can make the earliest mass, where parishes often do not have cantors, organists or choirs to "prolong" the liturgy? Also, every one of our parishes has weekday masses where, generally, little singing happens.

We can easily conceive of Catholic worship without music. So why have it?

Answering that question helps shed light on the particular ministry of liturgical musician, whether it is choir director, cantor, organist, composer, choir member—or even participant in the congregation. Catholic worship arose from the lived religious experience of the Jewish people who, throughout their whole history, used poems and music to memorialize the work that God accomplished in their lives. The singing itself became part of God's revelation. One of the earliest examples of this can be found in the book of Exodus, where, right after the decisive escape from the pursuing Egyptians over the Sea of Reeds, Miriam, Moses' sister, breaks into song: "I will sing to the Lord who is gloriously triumphant, horse and chariot he has thrown into the sea!" (Ex 15:1).

Scripture scholars tell us that this is one of the earliest parts of the Bible to be recorded, so ancient is the language that is used in this song. How did it get remembered? Why did it end up in the Bible? Because the song caught the historical and emotional experience of what God had done to free the Jewish people from their centuries-old slavery. This song so caught the experience of liberation that it became a refrain in the lives of the Jewish people. By singing the song again and again, the very moment of their liberation became vivid and powerful in their lives.

Liturgical music, in other words, captures a theological moment, and, through the emotional effects of the singing, enables someone else to enter that theological event spiritually.

In addition to the whole book of Psalms—150 songs of the Jewish people that formed their spiritual and communal background—the Jewish scriptures are filled with poems and hymnlike sequences in the works of the prophets and all of the wisdom literature. This body of music created the kind of environment that enabled the Jewish man, woman or child to feel a part of God's ongoing relationship with the Jewish people. More so than any Broadway show or popular recording, this body of music formed the deepest and daily religious references for the Jewish people.

In the New Testament we also find music—Jesus' singing with his disciples after the Last Supper, the hymns that Luke records as ways to remember the birth of John the Baptist and the incarnation of Jesus, the early church hymns in the letters of Paul (e.g., Phil 2:6 ff.) and the way heavenly singing organizes the book of Revelation, surely echoing the worship of the early Christian believers in Asia Minor.

There is a whole theology at work here, based on the incarnation, that is, based on God's using the very structure of our humanity to communicate grace. God is so pledged to doing this that God becomes one of us in Jesus, God's Word made flesh to come as our brother. All of Catholic theology is based on this central truth of our faith. God takes us so seriously that God becomes one of us.

What makes us human? Our human souls, we might say. But we know of our human souls by the actions that they empower in us—by our intelligence, our decision making, our anticipation, our ability to form relationships and, according to modern philosophers, in a special way through our ability to speak. Human consciousness, after all, can be seen in part as the ability we have to speak within ourselves. Speech is a special flowering of the human spirit and it thereby plays a special role in defining human nature.

We only need to think about the thousands of messages we get every day through every medium to appreciate the way words form the background of our human experience. These words have at least two aspects: They communicate information (as in, "Mary is sick") and also carry an emotional tonality that corresponds with our feelings (as in, "Mary is sick—and I feel badly about that").

Music emphasizes the emotional tonality of human communication, lifting into sounds the various emotions we have come to associate with certain experiences and certain words. It presses upon the extremes of human consciousness, gripping us with feelings, intuitions and connections that otherwise might be hidden or unrealized.

Music without words evokes various moods in us—the blah mood of Muzak or the excited mood of the first movement of Beethoven's Seventh Symphony. Music with words seems to draw powerful feelings from the words themselves. Country music fans exalt in the direct human feeling of the words-with-music, as do followers of some rock bands. Even rappers—who emphasize words more than music—get caught up in the beat and the mesmerizing quality of the rhythm of the music. Perhaps no form of music-with-words pushes the emotional tonality further than opera, in which whole themes emerge wrapped in powerful music and just-as-powerful lyrics.

Church music is not entertainment, because the point of entertainment is to induce the feelings that are themselves produced through the artistic work. In church the object is not simply to evoke feelings but to bring people into a more explicit relationship with God through the giving of themselves in worship. While feelings are not the object, they are a part of this giving of ourselves in worship. Music assists the whole process of worship by encasing in rhythm and tone the appropriate emotional dimensions of our spiritual lives. It adds delight to prayer, as our opening citation put it.

This does not happen, of course, exclusively through any one kind of music. We have all been touched by a Gregorian chant, by a translated German hymn, by what has been called folk music or by contemporary sacred music. Our being touched, by whatever music, only assists us in clarifying the dying and rising that is part of worship.

In worship, Christ's death and resurrection is made available to us spiritually. When we worship, we bring the dying and rising that is part of our human pilgrimage and relate them, in loving sacrifice, to God through Jesus Christ. We do this not anonymously or through a private mantra, but in the assembly, gathered by Christ in the Spirit, gathered around the table, an assembly that now feels itself in powerful ways through its common song. Singing helps worship by allowing the congregation to know itself, to be in touch with the range of its religious feelings, to clarify its relationship with God and to express that relationship in worship.

The ministry of liturgical musician, then, has a direct and powerful role to play in the evangelizing dimension of our eucharistic worship. It helps gather community; it helps renew the community; it helps empower community to that point of self-gift where, in love, we commit ourselves to God once again and go forth as his disciples.

Since the ministry of music is rooted in faith and discipleship, it takes on an explicitly evangelizing character.

How Music Ministry Evangelizes

"Not unlike preaching, the ministry of music can be considered a ministry of the word. As such, it plays a significant role in the formation of the religious imagination of the eucharistic assembly....Above all, music is a mode of evangelization par excellence." So wrote Father Richard Fragomeni, a priest of the diocese of Albany, New York, who holds a doctorate in liturgical studies from Catholic University. (See *Music Ministry*, published by the diocesan staff of the Diocese of Superior, Wis.)

To grasp the evangelizing power of sacred music, we go to the discipleship that is at the heart of all Christian experience and from which so many evangelizing qualities arise. As with so many ministries, discipleship naturally expands to the qualities of hospitality, witness, invitation and proclamation that characterize the spread of the Good News.

Discipleship is both a point of departure and a point of arrival. Since we cannot share something that we do not possess, discipleship must be the center and focus of the music ministry, which includes the music director, the instrumental musicians and the members of the various choirs. The group itself becomes a small Christian community as it meets, week after week, sharing prayer, scripture and life. If a music ministry does not propel itself by continuous entry into the mystery of the Word of God, it will lose its perspective and its ability to help a congregation enter the mystery of worship.

Music ministry must also exude hospitality, not only within the group, but to the entire faith community. Sometimes music ministers form a group unto themselves and are even in their own world—perhaps because they are more interested in music than in religious music. If a music ministry becomes closed to the congregation, or not welcoming of new members or new ideas or new ways of prayer, it becomes stagnant and life-draining instead of vibrant and life-giving to its members and to the congregation. Musicians or singers who are dour or doleful are the very opposite of the ideal joyful Christian community that is open and welcoming to all.

The musicians' expression of joyful enthusiasm and their deep faith commitment witnesses to the larger community. The way they live their lives, their priorities (including an enormous commitment of time and energy to rehearsals and liturgies), the way they treat each other, and the quality of their faith expressed in music becomes the silent witness of their faith.

Discipleship leads to proclamation, which sacred musicians do with particular emotion and fervor. Proclamation of the word through music is gift to the whole parish community. Hymns wonderfully and easily proclaim the life, death and resurrection of Jesus Christ. As the congregation joins the choir on Good Friday singing, "Were You There?" the crucifixion is made present. The Gregorian *Christus Factus Est* seems to suspend in time the gift of Christ in his dying and rising. When the processional hymn on Easter morning is sung with gusto and profound joy, the words, "Jesus Christ is risen today...alleluia," powerfully assert the Good News of Jesus Christ. Singing songs like "This Is the Day," "Seek Ye First" or "Whatever You Do for the Least of My People," we are learning and memorizing scripture. How many of us have resonated with Carey Landry's "I Am the Bread of Life," "...you shall live forever!"? Or felt the unifying power of chanting together the Lord's Prayer? We have responded to the beautiful hymn based on the call of Isaiah, "Here I Am, Lord," and, at a bilingual liturgy, have belted out, "Digo Sí, Señor—I Say Yes, My Lord." In all of this, we proclaim Good News and respond to it.

Music also serves as a marvelous invitational ministry. Music not only proclaims the word in all its power but aids conversion through its verbal and emotional power. When we sing "Come back to me with all your heart! Don't let fear keep us apart," the invitation is almost palpable. If evangelizers are facilitators of conversion, music ministers certainly can facilitate conversion through the tone, melody and invitation of their music shared and prayed. The great revivalists of our times have always known the power of the music ministry by having warm-up music for an hour or more prior to their preaching. And the power of music is also known during the initiation phase of evangelization, as new disciples are baptized, confirmed, united in eucharist and commissioned for ministry.

Seven Habits of Highly Effective Music Ministers

If music ministry will evangelize, some fundamental attitudes and habits can make the effect of this ministry all the more powerful. We offer seven habits that can increase effectiveness.

1. *Keep your mission in focus:* First of all, know what your mission is. As a choir, have you discussed your purpose? Why are you doing what you are doing? If your mission statement is not something like, "To foster prayer and participation in worship and to foster ongoing conversion," then perhaps it needs reevaluation. If additional singers or instrumentalists are brought in for special holiday services, make sure that they share the common mission of the group.

The particular focus of music ministry often comes out at special liturgical events, even though they may take much more time and effort. Weddings, baptisms, confirmation and funerals are prime times for evangelization, as are the Christmas and Easter liturgical celebrations—for the simple fact that these special events may be the only services many people attend. At a funeral mass a few years ago, for instance, many people were visibly moved by the supportive and uplifting music. Three inquired about becoming Catholics and one actually did. She reported that while she had been thinking about it for a while, it was the music that touched her heart and allowed God to speak to her personally that day.

2. *Be open to innovation:* In other words, don't allow yourselves to stagnate by doing the same things over and over or by buying into the "but we've always done it this way" syndrome. Part of the music leader's responsibility is to keep up to date on liturgical change, new pastoral music and current ecclesiology. This is the "student" part of musical discipleship.

3. *Work collaboratively with other parish ministries:* Just as your choir would be cacophonous without music sheets or direction from the choirmaster, the parish would be disharmonious if every ministry "did its own thing." Musicians are sometimes thought to be very "sensitive" and "persnickety" by other parish ministers. Experience shows that the musicians easiest to work with are those who are the most sure of themselves and most connected to the parish. They do not view suggestions or new ideas as threatening; they know who they are and are open to others in their ministry. The opposite also holds true—church musicians deserve the courtesy of other parish ministers.

4. *Be alert to the needs of the parishioners:* Music for liturgies must be singable. Most people love to sing and welcome the opportunity, but if all of the songs are new or complicated or technically impossible for the average parishioner to sing, participation will be greatly reduced. The congregation will descend to being an audience, resulting in the parishioners' need to worship through song going unfulfilled. What are seniors, youth or particular cultural groups looking to sing?

A sensitive music ministry means sensitive ministers. Since most choirs are seated either at the front of the church or to the side, choir members usually have a much better view of the assembly than those in the pews, who see the backs of heads for the most part. Alert and sensitive choir members can spot the parishioner with the quizzical look on his face during the homily or the person weeping in the fifth pew after communion. Of course, the musicians need to concentrate on their music and director while singing, but they have an ideal vantage point from which to observe troubled congregants during the rest of the liturgy. While the primary purpose of the choir is to minister through music, its ministry extends beyond music. An evangelizing musician can reach out to that person in the fifth pew and say, "I noticed lots of tears while we were singing. Can I help you?"

5. *Seek personal and communal spiritual renewal constantly:* Discipline yourself to regular prayer, scripture study, worship and community outreach. Begin each rehearsal with prayer and sharing, even if you must add additional time to your schedule.

One good way to do this is to ask each person to briefly share whatever burdens they may be bringing to the choir meeting (e.g., a sick child at home, pressure with career responsibilities, illness in the family, financial concerns). Not everyone may want to share each week, but just knowing that there is an opportunity to share is comforting to church musicians, who then know they are cared about as persons and not just for their musical talent. As the sharing of burdens continues week after week, the choir becomes its own support system, with members ministering to each other.

Social evenings, an annual retreat, potluck dinners and other enjoyable activities help build the sense of music ministers as a community.

6. *Encourage creativity:* As musicians are already highly gifted and talented people, they like to create. Go ahead, write and perform that scriptural operetta or new Christmas pageant. Offer new arrangements of old music; set "Just a Closer Walk with Thee" to barbershop harmony or "Faith of Our Fathers" as country bluegrass. Plan a concert as a fundraiser for the poor, using all of the group's individual and combined creative talents. Who knows? Maybe there is another Andrew Lloyd Webber in your midst!

7. *Don't take yourselves too seriously:* Are there perfectionists around? What is the final criterion for successful music ministry? A perfect rendition, or bringing people closer to God through worship? Evaluating your motives for being in the music ministry, strive for balance between egoism and altruism. Research shows that most people will not invest their time and effort in projects or causes unless they provide value and benefits to themselves, but this is never the primary motive for ministry.

Freed from obsession with perfection, in touch with the emotional side of religion more closely than most ministers, serving as a sacred musician can easily be the most enjoyable of ministries. Have fun! Musicians, most of all, can know the joy of the Good News.

Reflecting on Our Ministry

• Does our music ministry have a mission statement? If so, is it a primary motivational factor in our ministry? If not, consider having the musicians write a mission statement.

• Are those involved in church music becoming a supportive, faith-filled group rooted in discipleship? Are prayer, spiritual formation and ongoing conversion encouraged in our group?

• Are they sensitive to the needs of the parishioners, musically, spiritually and personally?

• How well do they relate with other parish ministers?

• Is the choir a clique or is it open to newcomers? How inclusive is the musical group?

• Do they work well with the parish liturgy committee? With the pastor and associates? With other ministries?

• Does jealousy or tension rule in the choir? How are the gifts of everyone encouraged and celebrated?

• Does music ministry lead the musician to evangelize?

CHAPTER SEVEN

Being a Catechist:
Being an Evangelizer

*[T]he definitive aim of catechesis is to put people
not only in touch but in communion,
in intimacy, with Jesus Christ:
only He can lead us to the love of the Father in the Spirit
and make us share in the life of the Holy Trinity.*
Catechesi Tradendae, #4

It's not always a pleasant arena, today's catechetical setting. Perhaps more than any other situation, catechetical efforts reveal unresolved tensions between people and the church. We offer a selection of some of these catechetical situations.

Example: For the fifth year in a row, Elizabeth has taught second-level religious education; for the fifth year in a row, she watches as parents debate whether their children will wear distinct first communion clothes and whether they will receive together or family style. She notes, sadly, that this conversation has drawn more energy from the parents than anything else.

Example: Andy wasn't sure he wanted to make confirmation, but his parents urged him to. Hardly any of his friends were in class with him. At sixteen, he had a lot of other things to do. To fulfill the requirements, he started going to mass more regularly and put in extra time "in service" at the nursing home. As the confirmation date approached, he found himself debating in his mind whether, after receiving the sacrament, he would want to continue going to church.

Example: Bill and Maria brought their children to religious education every week. When, during a conference with the teacher of their children, they were asked about weekly worship, they responded: "We each work and Bill holds two jobs; isn't it enough that we bring them to religious education?"

Example: Nancy went on retreat. During the retreat, the director suggested that the participants review their lives. Nancy, looking back at her twenty-three years, was surprised to observe that one of the high points was when, in seventh grade, during religion class, a prayer service that she was asked to lead helped her understand that Jesus truly lived today and was present in her life.

Each of these examples shows the opportunities and complications of catechetics today. Each of them, as well, shows the tensions of evangelization—how invitations happen, get set aside, get debated or receive a response. Some struggle, like Andy, with their personal stories still left incomplete. Others seem to have decided but, through their experience of raising their children in the faith, now are being challenged. Many of us can look back on the story of our own catechesis and see ever more clearly the Spirit's guidance.

Of all the tasks listed under the job description for a pastor in the Code of Canon Law (c. 528), the two that parishes accomplish most readily are the celebration of the eucharist and other sacraments, and the education of children and young people.

Naturally, then, ministries involving liturgy and religious education receive the most attention. Chances are excellent that, if a parish has the resources to hire professional parish associates, they will hire competent religious educators and liturgical ministers. As an obvious consequence, much of the parish's financial and personnel resources will go into these two areas as well. Of the two, however, our experience is that in many parishes religious education gets a slightly greater nod. Parishes seem to gravitate naturally around children. Were they to neglect this, the parents would raise up a storm to make sure their children are being attended to.

The attention that parents and parishioners generate falls for the most part under the category of "preparing them for the sacraments." Religious education often comes down to preparing children to receive holy communion or confirmation. Even in Catholic schools, where religious education can be given more consistently over more years, the reception of the sacraments still receives the most focused attention. A further consequence of this child-focused attitude is that the broad ministry of catechesis rarely reaches successfully beyond children.

Such natural tendencies in today's parishes, however, obscure the fundamental evangelizing dimension of religious education and the evangelizing role of the catechist. Only by recovering the power of evangelization in religious education can we keep this essential ministry of the parish from becoming narrowed or even distorted. A little looking back can explain some of the confusion that makes catechesis so fraught with tension.

The Legacy from the "Good Old Days"

Anyone in the upper end of the "baby boomer" generation or older had a fairly common experience of "being catechized," because we all received the same method of indoctrination through the use of the *Baltimore Catechism* in one or another of its various forms.

The catechism laid out some general ideas about God, the commandments, more elaborate points about morals, the sacraments—and the "last things," replete with rather vivid drawings of poor souls stuck in hell or clamoring to get out of purgatory. Catechesis clearly was a process designed to transmit content. Rote memory only emphasized more the content of the lessons. Day after day, classrooms with forty or more children recited together the catechism questions and answers, one by one, until they were all committed to memory.

Of course, those children with the better memories won the gold stars and the religion medals at the end of the school year. Children who did not have such great memories still received an indelible sense of religion as content to be memorized—or there would be serious consequences. This method of rote memory undoubtedly did not differ from the approaches used for other subjects at that time—the common recitation of the "times tables" or the capital cities of states or phonetic sounds or dates of the Civil War. These commonly recited lists formed rhythms that still resound in the heads of children educated before the Second Vatican Council. It would be foolish not to acknowledge how much this legacy of the *Baltimore Catechism* and its method of rote memory have continued to influence our thinking about catechetics.

Two of the most often expressed complaints—justified or not—that one hears in today's church go something like this:

(1) religious education (CCD) can never do in one hour what a child receives in Catholic school; and (2) children don't know their faith because the content has been obscured by all the "warm fuzzies" that distract us from religious education today.

Both of these complaints, upon reflection, refer back to the "good old days" and show how we continue, consciously or not, to try to replicate in today's experience what took place in those halcyon days. Even though this legacy of catechetics still holds implicit sway for many, no one ever asks why the early "baby boomer" generation, which was so extensively catechized by this method of rote memory, exited the church—or at least dispensed themselves from the need to practice their faith—in unprecedented numbers. Whatever was happening during those years, "making disciples" was not one of the unquestioned outcomes.

Without doubting the values of content and discipline, our holding on to the emotional feel of the *Baltimore Catechism* days might be making us slaves to dated and tarnished images of catechetics, images that we can subtly bring into the teaching situation. Looking at catechetics afresh, from an evangelizing perspective, might allow us, in our various catechetical ministries, to develop a complex of values that both define our roles and serve the needs of the students and church. This gospel perspective will also renew the catechist's understanding of his or her ministry.

Catechetics and Evangelization

In its most recent documents and teaching, the church has been urging Catholics to think of catechetics in the context of evangelization. In the 1997 *General Directory for Catechesis* published by the Congregation for Clergy, for example, the opening ideas collect themselves under the heading, "Catechesis in the Church's Mission of Evangelization."

The approach makes clear that the notions of catechesis and evangelization should not be completely merged. Evangelization has to "completely incorporate its intrinsic bipolarity: witness and proclamation, word and sacrament, interior change and social transformation." Its rich notion as the initial proclamation that calls to conversion should not risk being "impoverished" (#46). Evangelization, in short, cannot be collapsed, simply speaking, into catechesis.

But there is a dynamic relationship between evangelization and catechesis. The one implies and even demands the other. If the Christian faith is "above all, conversion to Jesus Christ, full and sincere adherence to his person and the decision to walk in his footsteps," this demands a "personal decision to think like him, to judge like him and to live as he lived" (#53). This is to speak about formation in Jesus Christ, about the development of the initial evangelical movement into mature Christian life. Catechesis builds upon initial evangelization to form the ongoing growth that Christian life entails. The *General Directory for Catechesis* says:

> [C]atechesis, situated in the context of the church's mission and seen as an essential moment of that mission, receives from evangelization a missionary dynamic which deeply enriches it and defines its own identity. The ministry of catechesis appears, then, as a fundamental ecclesial service for realization of the missionary mandate of Jesus. (#59)

There is a complementary role between the ministry of catechesis and evangelization: Evangelization is the ministry of the word that initiates, converts and incorporates a person in faith; catechesis, as an essential process in this ministry (#65), continues the formation of a person in faith—through study of the scriptures, a faith-filled reflection on contemporary times, an exploration of the meaning of liturgy, reflection on the individual events of personal life, spiritual formation and theological education (# 71). At the same time, the power of the initiating evangelization proclamation can and should be renewed throughout Christian life. "These [evangelizing] moments, however, are not unique; they may be repeated, if necessary, as they give evangelical nourishment in proportion to the spiritual growth of each person or of the entire community" (#49).

The *Directory*, when it talks about catechesis, has two guiding concepts in mind: first, it sees catechesis primarily as an adult experience (#59) and, second, it sees catechesis modeled on the baptismal catechumenate (also #59). Saying this does not in any way diminish the importance of catechizing children but simply points out that it is as adults that we primarily respond with human fullness to the import of God's Word and the church's teachings in our lives. Evidence of the widespread acceptance and success of the adult catechumenate is visible in virtually every parish.

So what about catechizing children? Isn't that what the modern church spends most of its time and money doing? Isn't this exactly what ties us up in knots and makes us feel that we are either accomplishing well or poorly the work of the church?

In his encyclical on catechetics, Pope John Paul II made some very powerful observations on catechizing children.

He explained that, in a general and basic way, evangelization precedes catechesis. But, he noted with particular emphasis, when it comes to the catechesis of children, evangelization and catechesis often occur at the same time! It is through the process of catechetics that some children, those whose faith is not nurtured in the home, receive the first, initiating, evangelizing messages of faith. "A certain number of children baptized in infancy come for catechesis in the parish without receiving any other initiation into the faith and still without any explicit personal attachment to Jesus Christ," writes Pope John Paul II (*Catechesi Tradendae*, #19). Catechesis has to concern itself with this initial formation and personal attachment.

In other words, the ministry of catechesis, when it comes to children, has to be viewed as directly analogous to what is happening in the baptismal catechumenate—people are hearing the Christian message for the first time in a meaningful way that is relevant in their own lives, and, with that proclamation, are drawn to come to a firm inner adherence of their whole selves to the person of Jesus Christ, to the God he revealed and to the church that he brings into community through the Holy Spirit.

This certainly changes most of the way that we view the ministry of catechesis in today's church—a ministry that is often shrunk down to the basic preparations we do for children as they prepare to receive sacraments. Rather, this preparation for the sacraments has to be viewed in that much larger framework of incorporating people into Christ in such a way that they become his disciples, that they come "to think like him, to judge like him and to live as he lived," to repeat the phrase used in the *Directory*.

Catechists do for children what members of the parish's catechumenal team do for adults in the process of the Rite of

Christian Initiation for Adults (RCIA): They help people in the process of conversion. They perform a ministry that brings people from questions and openness to faith to the maturity of discipleship.

All catechists, whether of adults or children, should have their framework shaped by that inherent missionary dynamic that gives this ministry its very reason to be. Catechetics is a dimension of mission; it either directly fosters or builds upon evangelization. It is a process of elaborating God's Good News in such a way that, through formation, Catholics become in today's world Christ's true disciples.

Discipleship and Catechesis

The ministry of catechesis, like all ministries, begins with discipleship. This dimension, heightened all the more because catechesis is the process of passing on discipleship from one to another, gives catechesis its primary evangelizing dimension. Those who catechize, whether volunteers teaching preschool children or directors of the catechumenate guiding those being initiated into the church, instill a sense of attending to the Lord in his Word and following the Lord by action. Unless catechesis is understood as a process of making disciples, it will inevitably decline into something like merely teaching class or simply socializing with peers.

From discipleship, as we have seen so often, arise the dimensions of witness, proclamation, attending to needs, invitation and empowering.

We have all known the difference between a "CCD teacher," who showed up for forty-five minutes of unprepared class, and a catechist, who drew from us ever deeper responses to our maturing grasp of God's Word. Perhaps we ourselves have felt those moments when a teacher in faith sensed something happening inside of us and asked us to stay for a chat. We have known the religious sister or brother who did not make us feel ashamed of difficulties at home and, even more, gave us strength to overcome those difficulties. If we are committed ourselves to following Christ with seriousness, we can undoubtedly remember when a religious leader or friend invited us to take a spiritual step that we had otherwise resisted.

Catechesis, the great process of building up the church, ultimately is quite personal. It replicates today the same energy that we so often find in the New Testament when someone directly receives a graced call through the lips of another—Andrew calling to Peter, Ananias touching Paul's blinded eyes, Barnabas talking to the Ethiopian, Jesus opening up the soul of the Samaritan woman.

If discipleship is at the root of evangelizing catechesis, how should we think of it?

One of the ways to understand discipleship is to look at the four basic sections of the *Catechism of the Catholic Church* inasmuch as they outline the components of catechetics and, as important, their interconnection. The *Catechism* itself is meant to be a resource book for bishops, pastors and catechists. One dreads the thought that the integrity of the *Catechism* will be boiled down to a word-for-word list of answers to be memorized. Nowhere in the process of writing or publishing the *Catechism* was this ever a guiding notion, or ever suggested for that matter. In fact, the *Catechism* itself resists this very thought.

But the fundamental pieces that make up the *Catechism* do form four foundations for Christian experience and, as such, provide a stable base on which to build an understanding of discipleship. Catechists can look at these four dimensions for insight into the kind of development they are called to experience themselves and the kind of development they are helping to instill in their "students."

1. The Creed

The "Creed," coming from the Latin word *credo* (I believe) is our common way of telling the story of our redemption, the *kerygma*, as it was called in the early church—the Good News of Jesus. It states the basic elements of the Christian story: our creation, our redemption through the death and resurrection of Jesus, and our participation in that redemption through the Holy Spirit and the church. Without hearing and accepting this "Good News," it is impossible to be evangelized because we are called to respond in faith precisely to this message of Good News. (The Latin word for "Good News" is *evangelium*, hence our word *evangelized*.) Everything else in our faith life will depend on our hearing and accepting this message of salvation—which comes about through the work of the Spirit of Christ—our belonging to Christ's community, our moral vision, our actions, our worship and our personal faith.

A catechist, then, *proclaims* the Good News of Jesus and its implications, as his or her first task.

2. The Celebration

The second major part of the *Catechism* is organized under those tantalizing words, "The Celebration of the Christian Mystery." When we hear the message of salvation, we celebrate it, as Christians have celebrated it for twenty centuries. *Celebration* means that, as a faith community, we proclaim together the story of faith and we participate together in the sacraments that bring about the Good News in our own lives. Every sacrament is a particular participation in the dying and rising of Jesus Christ; in every sacrament, the action of the story of salvation is "re-presented" again in a way that makes it active in our own lives, that makes it our story of faith. The New Testament and the unbroken experience of Christians tell us that being evangelized means inserting ourselves into the saving action of Jesus' death and resurrection through the sacraments. In the sacraments, Christ acts and the Spirit of Christ transforms our lives.

A catechist, then, *invites* people to experience Christ in the worship of the church.

3. The Life
The next major division of the *Catechism* is simply called "Life in Christ" and tries to indicate the result of our having heard the Good News and being touched by Christ's Spirit—our changed lives, our ongoing conversion, our moral vision (which is nothing else than the vision of Jesus) and our following of Christ's way of life, with the opportunities and sacrifices that it unfolds before us in our social settings, our workplaces, our families and our personal situations. While this section is organized, according to tradition, under the rubric of the Ten Commandments, it is hardly just about following laws. All moral action springs from the saving power of Christ's Spirit; all of it is built upon values and virtues; all of it is the product of God's love and our loving response in turn. Understood this way, moral life is not something we do to prove we are good enough to be saved. Rather, our growth in virtue is salvation itself taking place in us. Living as Christ lived is what "new life" is all about. Although we will never be perfect (and, therefore, will always need repentance and rec-

onciliation), striving for the perfect form of Jesus Christ is how we know that our evangelization is real and effective. Someone cannot be evangelized unless, hearing the Good News and receiving the grace of the Spirit, he or she begins to live the "new life" that St. Paul talks about (e.g., Rom 6:3 ff.)—death to sin so we can be alive in Christ.

The catechist, then, *helps form disciples* into living witnesses of redemption through graced actions.

4. The Spirituality

The final, interconnecting element in Christian disciple-ship is presented in the *Catechism* under the simple formula of "Christian Prayer." This does not mean that prayer has not been part of the other elements of a disciple's life—the Good News, celebration and new life. It means that prayer, deeply personal and deeply communal, forms the "interface"—if you will pardon a modern word—through which we grow as disci-ples. Prayer is the way God "formats" us to be followers, allowing us, through our personal experience, to appropriate in our lives the Good News, the meaning of worship and the import of moral growth. As human beings, we must attend to what is important for us. As redeemed human beings, prayer is the way we attend to Christ's Spirit in our own lives. Prayer unites, in a personal way, the Good News, the sacramental and moral life, into an unbroken human experience. Without prayer, we miss the meaning of the story, the mystery and the life; we never quite get it. We grab pieces of it, but it does not hold together as one.

The catechist *models and invites* disciples to life-giving and life-guiding prayer experiences.

We can see, from the cumulative presentation in the *Catechism of the Catholic Church* what discipleship means. The catechist invites and empowers others, on the pilgrim journey of faith, to become disciples by opening up the Good News, by celebrating the mysteries of faith, by discovering the saving power revealed in a new moral life, and by growing in prayer every step of the way.

This powerful vision of discipleship is exactly what the church is so often missing today. Catholics will accept themselves as parishioners and even as volunteers; but they do not consciously go on to the next step, to see themselves as disciples, as personal followers of Jesus, because their lives have been touched by his Spirit.

Looking at catechesis this way helps to erase some of those traces of the *Baltimore Catechism* legacy because our task is not to get children or adults to memorize things, but to help children grow up to be disciples and to help adults accept the discipleship that God calls them to through ongoing conversion.

This obviously means there has to be content, substance and material for disciples to learn; after all, the word *disciple* means "pupil." But it also obviously means that learning involves many simultaneous dimensions of Christian experience. We do not become disciples through the "classroom," even though we need wisdom to be disciples. We do not become disciples by following rules, even though we need moral strength to be disciples. We do not become disciples by some uniform and invariable "system" being applied to everyone, even though we cannot be disciples apart from involvement in a community of faith.

We become disciples by being evangelized and growing in that evangelization through the ongoing maturing that God invites us to. What would it be like if we catechists looked upon our "students" as codisciples with us?

An Evangelizing Catechesis

How can evangelization shape our catechetical ministry? Here, some clear directions emerge from our reflections on the church's understanding of catechetics:

- Catechists must understand themselves as disciples, constantly growing in their understanding of the Good News, its impact on Christian life and the personal commitment that is involved in being a disciple.

- Catechists have to understand themselves as evangelized people—and yet still in need of further evangelization—in order to communicate the fundamental starting point for catechesis.

- Catechists have to see their ministry as both a "calling" and a "teaching" ministry—calling adults, young adults, teens and children into community (and "wisdom" community) and helping bring that entrance about.

- Catechists can beneficially think of all their ministry as based on the Rite of Christian Initiation for Adults—as a process of making disciples who, in addition to the content of faith, find their lives enriched by the behaviors of discipleship. Catechists cannot divorce their own personal prayer and moral life from the ministry that they are trying to accomplish.

- Catechists have to insist that worship be part of the religious formation experience. Inserting religious "teaching" in the context of prayer, paraliturgical and liturgical experience, as that is appropriate, is a powerful way to build faith.

- Catechists of children can also see their work as involving the whole family and not simply the child they see. Providing resources for the family to grow in faith can be an important exercise of their ministry.

- Those who catechize children also have to help the parish see itself involved in the total catechizing of the whole community. This means more than our usually abortive efforts at adult education, with the usual fifteen or twenty participants. The ministry of catechetics cannot shrink down to the ministry we do for children.

- Catechists today understand that often it is the child who will bring the Good News home and end up evangelizing his or her parents. Making the most of such opportunities will only increase the power of the catechist's ministry.

- Catechists need not see themselves isolated in their ministry; they are part of a team of ministers who, through shared prayer and shared faith, reinforce each other in their catechetical efforts.

- Catechists will need to continue growing in their own understanding of the faith. Being involved in—and inviting others to—such efforts advance the environment of religious understanding of the whole parish community.

- Catechists can use the special opportunities that sacramental preparation offers without restricting their vision only to such occasions. How the sacraments integrate with the whole living of Catholic life remains an essential project.

- Catechists can resist playing into the "good old days" legacy and recognize the multidimensioned and holistic approach to religious formation that has to inform modern religious education.

Rome Wasn't Built...

Catechetics, because it is so important, can be viewed like the government or the public school system—a catch-all that is supposed to answer all our questions in the contemporary church. Every time a study is done, or an observation is made, or a complaint is raised, it's the catechetical personnel who have to suddenly come to a new insight, arrive at a new methodology or implement a new curriculum and, presto! everything will be suddenly perfect.

The old saying, "Rome was not built in a day," contains essential wisdom for us contemporary Catholics, so impatient are we (though we are hardly sure what the impatience is all about). Church life is not a list of problems with obvious solutions mindlessly applied. Church life is community—the interaction of many people, many needs and many visions, in the mystery of Christ.

No more can we look naively in the New Testament for the so-called "perfect church"—that hardly ever existed—than we can demand that our present church experience be ideal and perfect. Similarly, we cannot keep pointing fingers and wringing our hands about things, as if the Holy Spirit had left us orphans when Christ said his Spirit would never desert us (Jn 14:18; 16:13).

It is in our common pilgrimage, one step at a time, day by day, decade by decade, century by century and, indeed, millennium by millennium, that Christ builds up his body.

Seeing our catechetical ministry as evangelizing does not lay upon the catechist any more burdens than the ones inherent in the ministry itself. Catechists need not bite their fingernails in regret because they feel they have to recreate themselves as evangelizers.

Rather, an evangelizing vision, with its implications, can help catechists take a long-range view of their ministry, seeing the formation of children, youth and adults as part of the lifelong building up of the church that the Holy Spirit accomplishes. Evangelization helps us see catechetics as rooted in evangelization and directed toward discipleship. It is a vision of the greatest hospitality, welcoming others into discipleship as they take their rightful places among the daughters and sons of God.

That vision alone may help us be more patient with ourselves as we carry out our important mission.

Reflecting on Our Ministry

• What models of catechesis dominate the way I do my ministry? What are the benefits and liabilities of these models?

• In what ways do I deepen my own discipleship as a way of serving those whom I catechize?

• How does my image of catechesis transcend rote memory or the classroom or sacramental preparation?

• Do I see myself as an inviter in catechesis? How do I invite those I teach to deeper experiences or more mature faith?

• Is my catechesis directly related to the Good News? When I present the faith to others, does the basic outline of the story of faith bring power to my words?

• How do I teach Christian morality? If I use the commandments, can I get beyond images of "law" and "punishment" to a sense of moral life as the work of the Holy Spirit? How do I evaluate Christian behavior in the process of becoming a disciple?

• What role does prayer play in catechesis? In my life? In my ministry as a catechist? In those I teach?

• Do I feel isolated as a catechist? Where do I find the support of others? How is catechesis related to the work of the rest of the parish?

• How does my teaching reach beyond my "students" to their parents, their peers, their families, their environment? How do I help empower those I teach in their discipleship?

• How does my catechetical ministry take into account the needs and particular situations of those I catechize? How willing am I to show my care of others? How readily do my "students" learn to show care for each other?

CHAPTER EIGHT

Youth, Young Adults and the Good News

Youth must not simply be considered as an object of pastoral concern for the Church: in fact, young people are and ought to be encouraged to be active on behalf of the Church as leading characters in evangelization and participants in the renewal of society.
Christifideles Laici, #46

"I could not believe it when he asked me," she said. She, just turned sixteen, was talking about her parish priest. Over the years various associate pastors had started groups for teenagers and, over the years, these groups disintegrated as personnel and personalities changed.

Now there was a new priest, starting again. As she left church on Sunday with her parents, the priest asked her to consider joining the new group. As she related her unbelief that she would be asked, she turned up her nose and shaped her lips in complete distaste.

What was the problem? She really could not say, but she just knew it was definitely not for her. Life for her age group and for those a little older has gotten very complicated. It's like a new world, with its own code and rules, its own mode of interpretation and its own risks. Yet this is the world to which the church, particularly through youth ministers, would speak.

The universe of the adolescent has surely changed since the first baby boomers were making their way through the late '50s and early '60s. Popular music, which then only hinted at wildness and flirted with eroticism, has transformed itself many times over, such that excess and eroticism are almost commonplace in the world of entertainment. The children of working-class men and women, who at that time aped the family of Ozzie and Harriet, have morphed into today's youth, highly suburbanized or overly urbanized, expecting to succeed in college and a fine career—or expecting to fail as one more urban statistic, one more victim of drugs and violence.

The youth of the '50s may have borrowed some of the courtesies of their parents; today's youth appear to create their own culture with its own etiquette, its own values and expectations. In the '50s teens talked of sex and feared being "impure," whereas today teens seem to have hardly any fears at all, except the fear that they do not know what to expect from life or what life will demand of them. The dream of having a decent job, whatever it was, and living in a decent neighborhood satisfied the wishes of teens two generations ago; today one must have a *career*, and only the best can satisfy.

References to religion and church were strained, to be sure, for the youth of the '50s; the big question was, once children graduated from Catholic grade school, what percentage would continue going to mass? Even then, the sad answer was that only a small percentage would go, in spite of years of Catholic catechism. But at least religious references were picked up by the youth of yesterday. Today it is commonplace to talk about how "illiterate" Catholic youth are— teens, twenties, young adults; everyone born since the Second Vatican Council, it seems, gets swept into this great net of "Catholic illiteracy," more than a generation of young people who can barely articulate the outline of the creed, let alone explain why they believe anything, if they do.

Modern studies of the practice of faith indicate that, more than any other factor, the "cohort" to which one belongs predicts one's religious practice. The cohort broadly named "post–Vatican II" skews all the scores downward when it comes to church attendance, familiarity with traditional practices or basic church teaching, and acceptance of standard Catholic morality. In fact, when one talks about the inactive and the unchurched, chances are excellent that one is talking about a member of this younger cohort in the church.

For all the differences, though, between teens fifty years ago and teens today, all youth have one thing in common. Each seems to form its own universe. Each group of teens seems to define itself apart from its broader and parental world. Each develops its own style of clothes and language, music and behavior, which creates a general kinship among peers. It is hard to know where this kinship comes from since it is not likely that youth conspire to reinvent themselves every five years. Chances are excellent that much of the teen and youth culture is driven by media, which is to say, by commercial interests that purchase time on the media to create in youth their "need" for a certain look or certain style.

Apartness and Hospitality

It is the apartness of adolescence that seems to stand out most of all. Teens translate this personally into "no one understands me" and no amount of argument will convince a youth that anyone ever went through anything similar to what they are going through now. Indeed, maybe that is true, so eroded have the values behind today's culture become. The apartness also shows up in the "group-think" that makes youth protective of their world, even belligerent about it, precisely because it is theirs. To attack their world is equivalent to attacking them.

Ministry to teens and youth, then, must reckon with this apartness and all its ambivalence. Whatever benefits or liabilities come with the cohesive views teens create for themselves, nothing is going to make this cohesion disappear. Not only does a lot of energy go into checking out other teens to see what the group might be feeling; their whole world says that youth can survive only by doing this kind of checking, testing, comparing and evaluating. Some youth, to be sure, have it in themselves to rebel against most of this; when they do, however, they follow another code which just happens to suit the subset that rebels.

The apartness of youth does not stand as its own isolated statement. Rather it calls upon believers, who know that youth and young adults have an essential place among God's people, to discover what *hospitality* and *welcome* mean. Many youths may indeed turn up their noses and purse their lips in distaste when the parish invites; but at least they know they are invited and at least the possibility of response is there.

Youth ministers, empowering the parish to establish the rightful place for youth and young adults, have to create the forum for hospitality and welcome. To do this, naturally, they must look upon all the youth, one by one, with the particular gifts and needs of each, with an acceptance and sympathy that cannot be questioned.

Because youth ministers have to care for the needs of youth, they cannot mix those needs up with their own. Often teens and young adults are working out issues that may be still unresolved in the lives of some adults. These may be the very adults drawn to work with youth, the motive being their need to resolve something in their own past experience or to fulfill their own present needs. Unless the needs of youth are being addressed primarily for the motive of serving them, without inappropriate interference from the unfulfilled needs of youth ministers, the ministry has every chance of failure. Aside from possibly questionable behaviors by those entrusted to care for youth, the young people themselves will see that youth ministers are ignoring their own legitimate needs and using them to care for themselves. This only plays on and increases the vulnerability of the young.

In addition to their apartness, the other characteristic youth seem to have in common across the generations is their vulnerability. The up-front pain of a Ricky Nelson singing, "I'm just a lonely boy," would be too risky for today's self-conscious world of youth. But the frailty is still there, hidden behind the collective mania for this or that singing group, style of dress, tattoo or party.

Because of the apartness and the vulnerability that have come to typify adolescence ever since it became a separate state of life in the '50s, youth have their own universe. Under our noses, in our houses, on our roads and in our malls, youths consider themselves a universe apart, a universe in which the Gospel itself lives and longs to be celebrated.

The Gospel to the Culture

Because of the separateness with which today's youth view themselves, helping to celebrate the Good News of God in their midst has a paradoxical quality.

The often-used phrase, "Today's youth are tomorrow's church," expresses that paradox perfectly. The assumptions of the statement betray the attitude that the church belongs to the adults right now, and that tomorrow it will belong to the youth. That is, youth somehow do not belong to the church of today—that youth and the church are apart. Maybe if we play our cards right, they will take their place someday in the church, but not now.

How can we treat as apart people who live under our own roofs, who are objects of so much of a parish's yearly expenditure, who rightly merit so much of our care and concern?

It makes no difference whatever parish one visits, whether affluent suburban or impoverished urban, the same cry is heard: "We've got to save our youth, our young people," and the feeling is one of inaccessibility and desperation. Inaccessibility because the youth seem so distant and so alien. Desperation because we don't know what we can do to "keep them in the church" or "bring them back to the church."

Because of the way youth culture defines itself, it is tempting for today's church to think of youth almost as an alien civilization, speaking the same language but meaning something entirely different, holding on to its peculiarities with a vengeance, untouchable in spite of our desire to hold them and love them.

But such a view virtually and inadvertently writes youth out of the church and out of standard human experience. It distances the church from them as much as it subtly endorses their distance from the church. It doubts the power of the Good News to penetrate even today's generations, let alone those of the new millennium. It creates a vacuum where it believes the Good News cannot reach. With such a set of assumptions, no wonder Catholic parishioners feel desperate.

Youth may have a need to view themselves as apart, but that is hardly the prerogative of a church that calls itself catholic.

Youth Ministry

In one way, the culture of modern youth makes a direct appeal for evangelization. The culture, in subtle and overt ways, asks modern youth to dismantle most of the assumptions of their childhood. This process begins in junior high, speeds up in high school and reaches a plateau after high school. Changes in body call for, it seems, changes in everything else. The certainties of the world of parents and teachers comprise the very structure that has to be taken apart.

This process of leaving home—whether metaphorically or not—shows up in the early fights about friends, studies, staying out, dressing up, dressing down and doing things that make the youth "look like all my friends," as he or she will insist. It also takes the direct form of children deciding they no longer need to "go to mass" or "believe all that stuff." The result is a picture of youth slowly coming apart as they proceed on a journey to "find themselves," near the age of sixteen, and then, after a decade, finding "their lives coming together" as they settle down into a particular community, job or family situation.

The modern myth is that everyone has to wander off, doubt everything, rediscover everything anew and, in the process, he or she will discover the "true self."

Much as we can see that this myth contains utter nonsense, this is still the myth that we implicitly support every time we buy products that espouse today's worldview of "finding oneself." Of course, this abandoning of everything happens only in a certain respect because all the while youth are shaking off the accretions of their parents' world, they are using their credit cards, borrowing their cars, doing laundry in their basements and, in an even subtler way, slowly becoming like the parents they believe they are distancing themselves from.

This myth places a very clear challenge for the youth minister, particularly for the evangelizing youth minister: In the process of "leaving home" and "finding oneself," what place will the role of faith have? Another way to put this would be: evangelization for children happens as children mature. How can the maturing process itself be a point of faith?

It is very clear that for many people the time of their adolescence and young adulthood was exactly when they began to see the meaning of faith for the first time through their own experience, from their own perspective. The most typical conversion stories are those that occur when people are between eighteen and thirty, the very stretch that has been concentrated on so much in modern times.

Evangelization of youth, then, is the process by which the very factors of their own maturing come to be integrated with their deeper appropriation of the faith. In "finding themselves," youth can also "find God" and, surprisingly for them, the "God of their parents."

Theologically, this can be grasped by one of the key metaphors for evangelization: death and resurrection. Surely nothing seems further from the world of youth than death, but is not the growth from childhood through adolescence, and adolescence through young adulthood, and young adulthood through maturity, exactly a succession of deaths and resurrections? Youth is difficult because so many things have to be given up in such a short amount of time—physical changes, cultural shifts, alliances of friends, emotional stages, relationships with family and with various kinds of employment—so many aspects of a person's life have to be let go in order for the next phase to be able to begin. At a time when their very inexperience of life makes every change hard to put into perspective, each transformation calls for the ability of our youth to die and rise in faith, because the love of God and the grace of Christ remain constant despite all the transition involved.

The youth may not see these successive changes as theological events. It may appear to them all a matter of hormones, acne and mood swings. But such culturally driven interpretations of their lives need not hide what is actually happening: God is working in their lives to bring them to a greater level of mature discipleship. God is making them, even through the blur of puberty, more surely into his servants, witnesses and builders of the kingdom.

The evangelizing youth minister and all who work with youth need the patience and trust to let these changes happen, often without predictability, until they begin to be seen as the gospel reality that they are. The minister needs patience because the very process of maturing requires that the youth "put it together" in his or her life. To offer the space, the vision, the "Word," the community and companionship by which this integrating process can happen (and without which it cannot happen) is one of the great contributions that parishes and youth ministers can make for youth today.

The very vulnerability that characterizes youth asks for the Good News. The very insecurities that the culture induces (we're too fat, too skinny, too white or too dark, too tall or too short, too sexy or not sexy enough, too male or female, not male or female enough, never smart enough, never charming enough, never poised enough) call for the stabilizing message of God's unbroken love for us in Jesus Christ. When we realize that the followers of Jesus were approximately the age of today's youth and young adults, it opens up the experience of Peter, Andrew, Mary Magdalene, Mary and Martha to today's youth. In discussion with their peers and through personal reflection, the crisis points of the scriptural stories can become ways through which the crises of youth today can be brought into the light of the Gospels. Youth ministry creates the "space" in which this can happen.

On Their Own and Connected

Providing "space" is a pastoral way to address the sense of apartness that characterizes all modern experiences of youth. The natural differences in pubescent development become the cultural apartness that defines the cohort and even levels within the cohort.

Pastorally, then, youth need each other to be secure in their bearings in the larger world. The need for each other in that unique peer bonding that characterizes youth today translates into a world where their insecurities will be lessened, their exuberance put into context, their differences not judged and their gifts applauded and accepted.

Evangelizing youth means creating a certain kind of hospitality wherein youth can create their own space and be space for one another. While this may seem like a dreadful world to adults, and may even—if certain kinds of music are any indication—be a dreadful world from any point of view, when youth are allowed to be safe in this way with one another, they begin to unveil among themselves the values that underlie their idealism. Creating this world hardly means putting youth in a room by themselves and ignoring them; doing that will eventually earn the youth minister and the parish a large lawsuit. Creating this world means having a definite place and group that youth are invited to join. In that group, youth can surface their own concerns and their own leadership. In that world, youth start calling each other to responsibility.

The parameters of this "space" allow basic values to be upheld, values of a religious, social and personal nature. Youth ministers consistently have to help call youth to conversion in Christ, but there is no sure map or rigid recipe for this. Attending to the youth themselves, their needs and questions, and challenging the youth on the terms of their own experience will allow some method to emerge.

Key in all of this is keeping the youth connected to the wider world around them. It simply is not fair to youth to let them descend into their own world as if it were the universe.

Nor is it fair to the larger parish to deprive it of the gifts and ministry of the maturing Catholics who form the youth group.

This also is true of groups of young adults, who can seem as different and as isolated as teenagers simply because the parish so often revolves around married families, while everyone else is forgotten, particularly the young adult. As a result, they can band together to take care of their own needs and be embarrassingly unconnected to the larger congregation. When this happens, both the young adults and the parish suffer because parishes can only be faithful to themselves when they recognize the membership of all their parishioners.

When parishes keep their youth connected, they affirm the truth that youth are part of the church today, and not just some gestating mutant meant for a future church. When youth stay connected to their parish, then their evolution into service and ministry in the parish seems a totally natural progress. This helps give young people an alternative to the myth of "leaving home" and eventually "finding yourself." While being themselves and being with themselves, they still avoid the isolation that so threatens them.

Of course, given the way modern youth are assumed to "go off and find themselves," one of the key roles of parish youth ministry will be to form an ongoing bridge between teens and parents. Youth are notoriously reluctant to open up before their parents, yet, through the youth ministry, essential bonds with some parental system can be forged because of the absence of a sense of threat or manipulation. These connections can take the same structure as the rest of the parish: participation as ministers during liturgy, serving as music ministers, involvement with the poor or the elderly of the parish, service to children younger than themselves, catechetical activities among themselves and with others, and ministries that promote personal, spiritual growth.

In other words, discipleship. When youth ministry provides hospitality and space for a population that views itself apart and feels vulnerable, it gradually brings young people into relationships with the church, their families and one another within the structure of discipleship.

Friend to Friend

Just as the notion of welcome takes on special meaning when dealing with youth and young adults, so too does the idea of outreach, because, even more than most evangelizing situations, youth evangelization will be through peers, friend to friend. This is true both for teens and for young adults.

Many an anxious parent has lamented that they can no longer reach their child. "He's like someone different," they say. "She doesn't talk to me any more." When the call to invite people back to the church goes forth, almost every parent in the congregation cringes with guilt and frustration. They want to call their young back, they've been trying to call their young back, but the more they try, the more distant their children seem.

There are many reasons for this, the primary one being the obvious crossing of family dynamics with church dynamics. Often there is just too much history between parent and child, or between siblings, to allow them to effectively reach out. "I remember when you were in diapers." "You've nagged me all my life." "It's time for me to go out on my own, so just let me be." Today's culture does not offer us much rhetoric to defeat such disarming sentences. If one tries, the old "script" comes out, with the lines ingrained in each of the family members, lines that have been rehearsed during every argument since puberty began.

Parents should not despair if they are not the most obvious ones to reach their youth. Why? Because the overwhelming evidence is that youth most effectively reach out to other youth, and young adults most effectively reach out to other young adults. Hardly any contemporary campus ministry starts off the year without a nucleus of committed youth trying to engage all the returning and incoming college students. While many students remain impervious to these invitations, many others not only hear them but respond to them. Such entrées often make it possible for young people to reconstitute their faith in a new setting, from a new perspective of themselves as independent and committed people.

Youth ministers surely will have to do some outreach on their own. But their most effective outreach will be to empower the youth to call out to other youth, to get peers to work on their peer networks with the relationships and the language that young people can respond to.

Such peer-to-peer ministry does not have to take the form of self-righteous people turning to prey on the unrighteous. Youth need not reach out to others waving a Bible or a crucifix in front of their faces. Evangelization rarely happens this way. Youth have to come to trust their own experiences and relationships. Youth ministers can help youth get in touch with those experiences that have led them to be committed to Christ and the church; that can be a start. But then other youth will begin to respond, perhaps out of a variety of motivations. Maybe the youth program is the only "place" where urban youth can feel safe, being together without the pressure of drugs, alcohol or sex. If that is a motivator for youth, it can also be a motivator for youth who are not active or involved in church. As they mature, the motives will deepen.

Upon these peer relationships the evangelical values of faith, maturity, responsibility, commitment, growth and discipleship can be built. As in all religious experience, it is not the youth minister's job to determine exactly how the Spirit will work in the life of each child or within each friendship. Some youth will be motivated by fear, others by loneliness, others by a desire for service, others by a very clear and conscious relationship with Christ, others by the simple need to get out of the house! Youth ministers have to know that God works with many different motivators to pull youth together to be part of the church.

The real test for youth ministry is to challenge the peer outreach so that it is truly outreach. Youth and young adults are quite similar to the Catholics who are in our parishes. After they get together, it is all too easy for them to feel that "the parish is for me," and the "youth group is for our group." Such a sense of group identity, while intrinsic to the ministry, can also seriously distort it if the youth are not constantly called to cast the "net" yet wider, to their other friends and neighbors who perhaps are even more isolated, more needful of Good News, hungrier for lifesaving connections. Many are the youth groups that exert a lot of energy (often without the youth minister knowing it) to keep others out so that "the program can be our program." The evangelizing youth minister has to be especially attentive to any dynamic that makes the youth or young adult group into an elitist clique.

Youth Activities

Aware of the apartness and vulnerability that characterize this population, aware of the need to provide space and connections, and accepting the role of peers in gathering youth together, the youth minister has to craft a ministry that touches a range of needs and helps the Gospel grow among the young.

Often he or she has only some sense of those needs; attending to the youth and giving them a place to speak and organize will sharpen that sense. Yet youth often do not know what they are looking for. They can articulate vaguely a desire to get together or "to hang out," but it doesn't get any clearer than that.

The youth minister, too, does not have to compete with or re-create every initiative that already exists for youth in the area. If sports programming already exists, the parish does not have to go into the little league business itself. If outlets for art and drama are available for youth, the parish does not have to provide the resources for activities such as these. In fact, sometimes, providing these resources outside the context of faith can be an outright distraction to the evangelizing efforts of the parish. How many CYO programs have provided softball or volleyball, with these programs forming a shell to keep the youth from connecting in anything but a superficial way with the faith community?

The truth is that a variety of efforts has to happen in the area of programming and, shaped correctly, these can create an evangelizing spirit in the ministry.

Consider the need for *socialization*—the capacity for young people to be together with dignity, respect, poise, responsibility and appropriate autonomy. This may appear, at first, as a rather unevangelical step, but the Gospel only happens in community, and community is built upon the human dynamics that allow people to be together constructively. How often did Paul have to call his communities to reflect on their basic communal dynamics in order to reveal the call of Christ to them?

Consider, too, the need for *service*—youth, like everyone else in society today, tends to be self-absorbed and insecure. But youth, perhaps more than most segments of society, have an idealistic yearning for service, to help build a better world, "not to make the mistakes that our parents made," as some might put it. The ability to serve opens youth to those wider worlds beyond themselves that are, in fact, the very nutrients they need for their own growth. Even within the parish, opportunities for service abound—youth, for example, in caring for younger children and in trying to impart their values, discover what their own values are. Service to the poor, the elderly, the Sunday congregation—many obvious ways of branching out in service become immediately obvious. Beyond the parish, too, lies a whole range of needs that call for the service of young people. The key here is not to ask the youth to do more than they are capable of doing, not to expose them to difficulties that will only make them feel like failures. Youth need to be supervised, in the best sense of that word, as much as any minister needs supervision.

Consider also *faith sharing*—the capacity of youth to talk about their struggles and experiences of faith with each other. Often this can happen best among personal friends, but youth ministers might also discover ways to help young people share with each other in safe settings without raising the embarrassment level. Encouraging the stronger youth to share in free and open ways—and discouraging the "bullies" from dominating the session—can provide just such a safe setting. The key to this will be the sense of community (socialization) that has been built up among young people in the group. Youth ministers must never forget that some people are just very private. No one's boundaries should ever be transgressed.

Consider, in the area of faith, *meetings with other youth groups*. Some of the most powerful witnessing that the world receives today comes from youth and young adults coming together as a large group to express their faith in a communal service or event. All the hand-wringers were completely thrown, for example, when hundreds of thousands of Catholic youth came to Denver at Pope John Paul II's invitation. The very gathering of so many gave everyone permission to be more open with his or her faith. Youth ministers will have opportunities from the diocese or regional youth conferences for gatherings like this. Youth ministers, with their youth, can help create such opportunities for nearby parishes or even for the whole local church.

Consider, too, *renewal programs* for youth. Nearly every diocese has a variation on "Teens Encounter Christ"—a Cursillo-like weekend experience—that has brought about powerful change in the lives of youth. Similarly, national efforts to reach youth can be brought down to the local level—programs specifically designed to touch young people. The more that youth can be involved in searching out these programs and helping them to work in their area, the more successful they will be. Youth ministers in this area need to be sure not to let one or another of these programs become a crutch for their own ministry. No program will make sense to youth unless it arises from the context of their own faith community and, in turn, provides ongoing reinforcement for that faith community. Young adults have often "flown" at an extraordinary renewal program only to "crash" when they return home and realize that life cannot be like the idealized experience they had.

Through a balance of approaches and opportunities, youth ministers can accomplish truly wonderful things with the young. Open to the variety of their young people, not put off by elements of the "youth culture" that are hawked in the media today, and open to the wide range of ways in which youth seek and discover the values of Christ, youth ministers can help the lives of the young be deeply touched and, in the process, help the life of the parish be touched by the lives of its young people.

The issues and directions that have been identified here are not really different from those identified with other ministries in the parish that have the power to evangelize. While hospitality has to play a larger role, discipleship, witness, proclamation, concern for others, community and attention to real needs are the dynamics by which evangelization happens among the young. The evangelized youth minister rejoices when the Good News leads youth to take on these same qualities.

Indeed, the greatest accomplishment of youth ministry is when the young people come to see themselves as ministers able to bring the kingdom of God into the lives of their friends and families. This is part of what Pope Paul VI meant when, in *On Evangelization in the Modern World*, he talked about "apostolic initiative" (#22)—that precious moment when the evangelized themselves become evangelizers. Youth ministry is hardly what "we do for them." It is what God's Holy Spirit empowers the youth to be able to do for each other and for the world. This "apostolic initiative" can happen if parishes stop thinking of youth as strange creatures from an alien world, as problems to be managed, as candidates for a sports league or as potential for a future church yet to be built. It happens when parishes come to see their youth as already containing the capacity to help bring the kingdom of God into reality—their reality, the parish's reality and the reality of today's world.

Reflecting on Our Ministry

• How does my parish look upon its youth? How do I? What place do they have in the parish community?

• How do youth view themselves? What kinds of groups form among youth and young adults? How cohesive or disparate are these groups?

• How would I identify the apartness and vulnerability of the youth I am trying to serve?

• What kind of hospitality does the parish provide for youth and young adults? What kind of "space" is reserved for them? How does the parish react to the meetings of youth and young adults?

• How do young people connect with the wider parish? How does my ministry make that connection possible?

• How do I encourage peer-to-peer outreach among the young? How effective is it?

• How much respect for the maturity of young people do I show? Are young people empowered by my ministry to serve each other?

• What kind of programming do I sponsor for youth? Do

young people have a say in its formation? What are the faith elements that are present?

• How do I encourage groups of the young to reach out to other youth and young adults? How do I keep these groups from becoming closed and inward-looking?

• How do I get supervision for the inevitable deep issues that arise in my ministry? How do I keep perspective? How do I serve as a professional in the lives of the young?

CHAPTER NINE

The Pastoral
or Finance Council:
Administration
as Ministry

The parish is the most fitting location
for carrying out these [evangelizing] goals because
the parish is where most Catholics experience the church.
It has, on the local level, the same commitment
as the universal Church, with the celebration of God's
word and Eucharist as its center of worship.
Go and Make Disciples, Part II

It began as an annual event, a retreat day for the pastoral council. A dozen laypersons sat around the large table, along with their pastor. They looked as if they had gone through this many times before, each with a slightly strained look that even the first-time members managed to have.

As the day unfolded, however, it turned out not to be a repeat of past retreats. One member raised his hand, and a second followed with her comments. He asked the group when they were going to face up to the plain and undeniable issues that faced the parish. All their meetings and all the constitutional machinery behind the pastoral council did not seem to give them the ability to deal with the basic reality of their parish life. There were agenda, reports, announcements, but nothing seemed to change.

Everyone looked to the pastor, who looked right back at them and said: "I'd certainly like the pastoral council to deal with the issue of how we, as a bilingual parish, can be one, unified community. How do we do that?"

Suddenly it was no longer a repeat of the past. Suddenly, the pastoral council felt free to go about its basic business and, in the process, discover how to make its parish community, filled with so much promise, more unified and evangelizing.

As important as the ministry of serving on the pastoral or finance council is for the whole vision of the parish, it is not an easy ministry; unfortunately it is not one that many Catholics eagerly undertake. How many times, for example, have parishes had elections (if that is the discernment method a parish uses) to the pastoral council and there were barely enough candidates to fill the open positions? How many times, in fact, have parishes suspended these elections because there were so few candidates that the parish just accepted all the applicants as new members of the council?

While the finance council does not often have the same publicity or election process because it involves technical knowledge about money that few parishioners feel they have, nevertheless pastors often have to go hunting for parishioners to serve on this council as well.

Why the reluctance for a ministry so vital to the parish's life? Examining this could be instructive.

An Encompassing Ministry

An examination of the factors that make Catholic laypeople hesitate to get involved with these ministries inadvertently reveals the importance of the ministry. We'd like to concentrate on two of these.

The first factor is a deep sense of unworthiness on the part of the parishioner. Because parishioners instinctively know how important their service on the pastoral council is, they do not feel inclined to put their names forward or to accept the suggestion of their parish leadership to serve.

"I can't do that," the parishioner automatically answers. "I don't think I can serve that way." And then the reasons will often follow in this manner: "I don't know the parish well enough." Or "I cannot accept all the responsibility." Or "There are so many others who can do this better than I can."

By these and similar answers, Catholics show the sense of importance that they invest in these parishwide min-istries. They know that serving on these councils means serving the core needs of their fellow parishioners—the need for a communal vision and a consistent effort to carry out that vision. They know it means serving the needs of all the parishioners, even needs the parish would rather ignore. It's no wonder Catholics are intimidated.

The second factor is time. Catholics today are so busy with their work and their families, that they feel the time involved in serving on these councils will simply be too much. One young man with a young daughter and a second child on the way sat calculating what was being asked. It was not only to serve on the pastoral council (one meeting per month), but also to serve on a committee of the council (another meeting a month), to get involved in the activities that the council might set in motion (at least one other meeting a month) and to be a representative for the diocesan association of pastoral councils or the diocesan pastoral council (another meeting a month). That kind of schedule, along with all the other demands on his life, seemed to take all his evenings away.

Even the finance council, which usually meets once a month for a fairly predictable hour or hour and a half, has its hidden time-consuming side. How about meetings with diocesan officials over the budget or a projected loan? Or meeting with the building committee when a foyer will be enlarged or an extension added to the school? Or interviewing various people who wish to help the parish invest its small but precious resources? Or sitting with various staff and committee members when it's time to put the annual budget together? Or crunching the numbers late into the night when the pastor gives his annual report to the parish?

The two factors of scope and time show the level of commitment that is being asked of lay men and women as they serve their parishes on these vital committees. To be asked to serve this way, by pastor or parishioners, is nothing less than, to use biblical imagery, to be called.

Serving the parish in the basic way that these ministries demand means that those who so serve must themselves be evangelized. One cannot serve the parish, a community of disciples, unless one has the same vision oneself. The credibility to call the whole parish to witness, proclamation, sharing of gifts, hospitality, concern for others and deeper community comes from living these traits oneself.

Parishes can always hire management or finance experts. Guess what these experts would ask first of a pastoral council? They'd ask what the vision of the parish is, what it saw as its core reason for existence, as its fundamental mission. Only a pastoral and finance council that sees Gospel at its heart can provide the fundamental vision from which all its commitments will arise. Expertise, then, is secondary. Vision comes first—a vision that springs from living and sharing the Gospel.

A Call to Evangelization

Precisely because serving on the pastoral or finance councils of the parish is such an encompassing mission, it deeply involves every Catholic willing and able to serve this way in the mystery of evangelization, in the process of salvation whereby, dying and rising in Christ, we gain entrance into the Lord's kingdom.

That may well sound pretentious and even ludicrous when reports still come in about pastoral councils spending almost an entire meeting trying to decide whether to repair or replace the aging snowblower or what exact shade the new rug in the parish center will be. Yet when we see what serving on these councils asks and presumes, we find we are far from the minutiae that often derails the ministry of some pastoral councils.

A perspective on this kind of ministry might well come from the often-repeated narration of the multiplication of bread, one of the few stories presented in every single Gospel (twice in Mark)—the feeding of the multitudes. We hear that story and always get hung up on the question, "How did the bread get multiplied?" when the point of the story is the wonder of how the ministry of Jesus gets multiplied through his empowering of his disciples.

We know the story's outline: how Jesus had been preaching all day and the people were spellbound; how the disciples suggested that Jesus let the crowd go because it was late and they would have to buy food for the trip home, and how Jesus shocked his disciples by saying, "You give them something to eat" (see, e.g., Mk 6:37). The disciples were stunned by Jesus' suggestion, observing that two hundred days' wages would not be enough to feed such a crowd.

But in the face of their hesitancy, Jesus has them put the crowd in order, "in groups on the green grass," as Mark puts it (6:39) and, having offered the blessing, tells the disciples to distribute the bread. In other words, he gets the disciples to organize and take part in his own ministry. He empowers them to feed people because of the food that he has provided for them. We feel the amazement of the disciples: "All ate and were filled, and they collected twelve baskets of the bread and of the fish" (Mk 6:43).

This kind of participation in service is not new; in fact, some of the narration of the multiplication of the bread has the same feel as Moses' decision, on the suggestion of his father-in-law Jethro, to select seventy elders to help Moses give justice to the Jewish people as they begin their trek through the desert (Ex 18:13–27). God is not stingy with gifts—gifts to empower people in the community to help the community be its fullest.

It probably would also surprise many modern people, with our suspicion of authority and supervision, to see Paul list "administration" as one of the gifts of ministry that the Spirit has poured down upon the church (Rom 12:6 ff.). Paul saw the church, the body of Christ, as the gift of the Spirit; along with the church, all those elements needed for the church to thrive and grow would also be given.

The pastoral council today has exactly that role, the service of the body of Christ in order that it might thrive and grow. Like the first disciples, the pastoral and finance councils have to set aside their worries about how things can be accomplished and whether there will ever be enough, in order to enter into the mystery of abundance that Jesus always shows his church. The abundance is all the gifts that God pours out upon his community of disciples and the depth of faith to which God leads all those who trust in him.

"You give them something to eat," says Christ. In saying this to those who minister in the running of the parish, Christ is inviting Catholic men and women today to acknowledge how deeply they are called and how closely they are identified with his own gift of ministry. In recognizing this, they also recognize how God's gifts of ministry have been poured upon so many. The disciples, like the apostles of old, make sure that all of these gifts, distributed by the Spirit, are used, recognized and celebrated.

Members of the finance council in particular are called to recognize the abundance of God even in the material sphere because there, today more than ever, we are tempted to mistrust the generosity of God. We are tempted to think that "You give them something to eat" means that God will not take care of us and, therefore, we have to develop miniempires of financial security in order to provide. One more fund-raiser. One more pitch for money. One more hike in the tuition.

Yet none of us can read Luke's Gospel, with his call for utter dependence on God and utter freedom from preoccupation about "things," and not see that this speaks to the deepest question of our evangelization—how our riches and trust are in God and not in ourselves. "Ask and you will receive, seek and you will find, knock and the door will be opened....For if you, evil as you are, know how to give good gifts to your children who ask, how much more will your heavenly Father give good gifts, the Holy Spirit, on those who ask?" (Lk 11: 9–13). Matthew tells us explicitly not to worry about what we eat, drink and wear because that's what unbelievers do. "Seek first the kingdom of God and all these will be given you besides" (Mt 6:33).

Given these words of Jesus, challenging us to the greatest trust in the goodness of God, those who serve on the finance council and the pastoral council must be deeply grounded in stewardship—acknowledging that we are called to live generously because of our trust in the generosity of God. None of this calls for fiscal irresponsibility. None of this means we have to erase the spreadsheets from our computers. It does mean that we cannot talk credibly about the resources of the parish, personal or financial, unless we do so from the perspective of Jesus, from the viewpoint of one who always sees the loving hand of God stretched open toward us with all the gifts that we need.

Serving in these ministries, then, means that we must be evangelized into that particular ministry of Jesus that springs from his relationship with the Father of heaven.

When Jesus talked about God as "Father" he was not jumping into modern gender politics; he was offering us the profound symbol of an ever giving, ever faithful and ever loving God, one whose divine presence provides the context of strength without which we cannot be disciples.

"Ask and you will receive," says Jesus. When you receive, then you know you can "give them something to eat."

Rooted in these gospel virtues of openness and trust, the ministry of serving the parish in its administration has the ability to call the whole parish community to live out its evangelizing mission.

Ministries That Evangelize

If the service of the parish community as members of the finance and pastoral councils demands a clear commitment—a commitment that springs from their personal evangelization and call to ministry as well as their particularly dedicated service to the parish community—it is also a ministry that calls all the parishioners to evangelize. It provides the essential vision by which evangelization is possible.

People with a high level of commitment are called to serve on these parish councils in order that the parish might be, without hesitation, the community of faith that God calls it to be. God asks much of those who serve in these ministries because these ministers will, in turn, ask much of a parish.

While an elaborate history of the parish might be instructive, it is enough to go to the section on parishes in the Code of Canon Law to begin to appreciate the kind of ministry these pastoral councils have to cultivate. The definition of parish in the code has two basic elements: (1) it is a stable community and (2) the celebration of the eucharist is at its heart. (Canon 515 defines the parish as "A definite community of the Christian faithful established on a stable basis within a particular church." Canon 528 details the place of the eucharist in the parish.) These two notions give, in themselves, important leads to the kind of ministry that must happen on the part of parish leadership.

First of all, a parish is a eucharistic community. Eucharist is at its heart. This means that the celebration of the Word of God and the sacred sharing in the body and blood of Christ form the fundamental spiritual architecture of the parish. It must be a community that lives by the Word of God—and by the ongoing appropriation of the Word through prayer, reflection, teaching and tradition. The church lives to proclaim that Word; the church lives by hearing that Word.

Along with its life in the Word, the parish is a community that gathers in unity around the table of Jesus—feeding on his very life through the reception of the sacred bread and wine through which Jesus becomes intimately present to parishioners today. This is a table of unity, for we all approach the one Lord and have his one life circulating among us in the eucharistic meal. It is also a sacred table, for when the community eats the food of Jesus it says it is united with Christ, united with each other and committed to living that unity. Third, it is a generous table, not set for the elite but for everyone who truly searches for Christ. It is a table where the bread is broken and the wine of Christ's blood is shed for all. This means that the eucharist is not merely for those who gather, but is meant for the world. It places, on all those who partake, the obligation to help Christ's love reach the world through their personal lives.

The second element of the definition calls for stability. The community formed through parish has to endure. Parish community does not appear and then disappear. It is not a flash in the pan. Rather, it abides as a community with a history, a purpose and a mission. It is like other communities that abide—such as families and religious congregations—which need something more than intense and occasional experiences.

Enduring, abiding and continuing in time mean that long-term and subtle relationships have to develop. While there will surely be high and low moments, the endurance of the community calls for more mature and nuanced structures. It calls for more long-term attention to the vital undercurrents of a community. An abiding community goes for decades and, in the case of parishes and religious congregations, potentially for centuries.

These dimensions of parish—its rootedness in the Word and in the table of Christ, along with its long-term endurance—demand a vision, a perspective that keeps the parish keyed into its essential nature and helps the parish escape preoccupations that may distract it from its nature as a faith community rooted in the eucharist.

The maintenance of that vision belongs to the pastor and pastoral staff; it also belongs to the pastoral and finance councils. These councils exist to serve that vision. Unless that vision is maintained, the parish will lose sight of its own purpose. Once that vision is maintained with power and clarity, it frees the parish to be its evangelical self.

Consider the following tasks that a pastoral council has to undertake if it will serve the parish:

- It must keep the Word of God central in the parish's life and call its parishioners to make the Word of God central in their individual and personal lives.
- It must make the eucharistic gathering on Sunday a celebration of the salvation that Jesus accomplishes through the Holy Spirit.
- It must enunciate again and again the implications of the body and blood of Christ. First among these is the call to holiness, for we approach the Lord's own body and blood to take him into our very selves.
- It must articulate just as clearly the empowering mission that comes from celebrating the eucharist—that we are sent forth as disciples to bring the Word and the Body to the world.
- It must elaborate on all the other ministries that arise because of the centrality of the eucharist—the catechesis, the proclamation and celebration ministries, the welcoming and inviting ministries, the service ministries, the spirituality and growth ministries that the eucharist needs for its vitality and effectiveness.
- It must continue to call the parish community to be faithful to its own mission—to be a community of the saved who call others to the salvation of Jesus Christ.
- It must work to make this community an abiding one, "stable" as the Code of Canon Law puts it, through bold and prudent vision, helping the parish stay free from anything that threatens it, particularly anything that would diminish its central mission.

The members of the finance council obviously must have a vision similar to that of the pastoral council. It, too, serves the entire parish and serves the basic purpose of parish: to insure the stability of the community that has the eucharist at its heart. Making this possible, with a view to the material and financial requirements for stability, the finance council has to match the resources of the parish to its basic mission.

How we use money shows our priorities. While obviously providing for a building and its maintenance is an undeniable dimension of the finance council, its most important work probably consists in funding those staff positions and ministries that reveal the priorities of the parish community. A parish that lines its walls with Italian marble while neglecting the needs of youth or failing to lead its people to attend to the Word of God more deeply, fails in its mission, fails the parish and fails the reign of God.

Important among the basic tasks of the finance council are:

- Keeping the parish clear on its priorities.
- Placing the need for resources in the broader context of trust in God.
- Calling the parish to stewardship, the gospel use of its resources in generosity and openness.
- Helping the parish see ways to fund its important positions and projects.
- Being examples of the generous stewardship to which they call others.
- Preventing the parish from being blind to the needs of others because it is obsessed with its own needs.
- Insisting that the parish maintain service and care of the poor at the heart of its commitments.
- Building cooperative bridges with other church groups that depend on scarce resources, particularly the school and the local (arch)diocese.

The major work of the pastoral and finance councils involves being faithful to the evangelizing vision of the parish and making it possible for the parish to be a consistent community of evangelizing gifts. How can the parish be faithful to its deepest vision unless those who are charged with counseling the pastor project and protect the essential mission of the parish community?

While these councils are advisory and never absolve the pastor of his responsibility for the parish, over the years it has become clear that pastors come and go, but the parish community, with its mission and vision, has a remarkable ability to transcend these changes. The more clearly these councils can fulfill their ministry from a profound and spiritual vision of parish, the more certainly they assure the future ministry of their community.

Tips for Serving on Pastoral and Finance Committees

When we are invited by our pastor or parish community to serve on these important committees, we receive an invitation to live more deeply the servant ministry of Christ. We are invited to be more deeply evangelized, not merely because of the greater sacrifice that is asked of us, but also because of the sheer importance of these ministries. How can those who serve on these councils serve more fruitfully? Here are some suggestions:

- See that your council is a council rooted in prayer and discipleship.

- See that your council grows in its own sense of community and service.
- Help your council see the place of the scriptures in understanding its work.
- Make sure your ears are open to everyone and your eyes are focused on the neediest in your community.
- Insure that your council operates from a clear and evangelical mission statement of the parish.
- Be willing to ask the deeper questions and to review the parish's mission and purpose periodically.
- Only participate in those actions that further the unity of the parish, its sense of binding love in the Holy Spirit.
- Live personally by the same principles that you ask of others.
- Support your pastor in his strengths; strengthen your pastor in his weaknesses.
- Make sure that you allow many others to become involved in service and not monopolize ministry for yourself. Foster the evangelizing vision behind all other parish ministries.
- Be a witness for the unchurched persons and the inactive parishioners who also deserve the full attention of the parish.
- Keep the purposes of God's Word, the sacraments and growth in discipleship at the uppermost of the parish's agenda.
- Support the creation and funding of an evangelization commission.

It's hard to read the letters of Paul without seeing how he depended on a network of others who worked along with him and made his ministry possible. He often refers to his coworkers and supporters: Silvanus, Titus, Timothy, Phoebe,

Lydia, Philemon, to name just a few of those many who formed the network of his missionary life. None of us lives our Christian lives alone; we need others and we need others to support us on the journey.

Today's ministers who serve on pastoral and finance councils do work similar to Paul's associates. They make community possible; they make parish happen. Their vision encompasses that of all the ministries and ministers in the parish, providing vision and resources, both guiding and being guided by the parish community.

Reflecting on Our Ministry

• Does my parish have a vision? What are its key points and priorities? Do I know that vision? Has it been reviewed recently?

• How do I go about serving the needs of the entire parish? What groups am I prone to listen to, and what groups get less attention from me?

• What sense of discipleship exists on the council?

• How are our meetings organized? What takes up most of our time and energy?

• Do we empower our parishioners or do we instead serve as the default committee to do everything? How do we challenge our brothers and sisters to greater discipleship?

• What is our relationship to the pastor? To the bishop? To other ministries and committees in the parish?

• What kinds of people tend to be chosen to serve on our council? Is the base of those who serve broad enough? Deep enough?

• How do we resolve conflicts? What kind of spirit is engendered in the parish?

• Do we see our ministry as evangelizing? Do we see evangelization as the fundamental mission of our parish?

CHAPTER TEN

Social Ministers: Good News for the World

Sacred Scripture continually speaks to us of an active commitment to our neighbor and demands of us a shared responsibility for all of humanity. This duty is not limited to one's own family, nation or state, but extends progressively to all mankind, since no one can consider himself extraneous or indifferent to the lot of another member of the human family. No one can say that he is not responsible for the well-being of his brother or sister (cf. Gn 4:9; Lk 10:29–37; Mt 25:31–46).

Centesimus Annus, #51

Imagine the activities of a parish organized in the form of something like a bull's-eye target. In this way we can imagine the center and we can imagine the outer edges. Certainly in the center are those activities which, regardless of the parish's size or location, regularly occur: the celebration of the mass and the other sacraments; preparation for the other sacraments and religious education; and, perhaps depending on the specific financial status of a parish, either few or many activities to raise money.

Just outside the center are those activities that arise from the basic organization of the parish. Parish staff and pastoral associates, receptionists, secretaries, ministers of one sort or another, activities for seniors or youth—all of these are fairly common. Depending on the demographics of the parish and whether the parish sponsors a parochial school or not, the bulletin will clearly lay out another level of obvious activities.

With the image of the target in mind, we can reflect on our own parish's involvement with and commitment to the social ministries that flow from the gospel message—its service of the poor, the marginalized, those forgotten in the middle-class bubble in which most Americans live. Where would the social ministry of any particular parish fall on the imaginary target?

In many parishes, service of the poor is clearly visible. But, by and large, it is done only by a handful of people under specific situations. In some parishes, service of the poor and proclamation of the Gospel to the world through deeds beyond the parish's own turf remain largely invisible, done perhaps by the priest whose doorbell rings at 10:00 P.M. or even by the parish receptionist at her or his discretion. As a result, the service of the poor is near the wider edges of the target, far from the center, at the periphery of the parish's attention.

At the Heart of the Good News

It is surprising, however, that the ministry of a parish to the poor and the wider impact of the Gospel on the world lies far from the center of most of today's parishes. No one who looks at the Gospels themselves can imagine the prophetic actions of Jesus—particularly extended to the poor and marginalized, the isolated and wounded—as not at the center of the gospel proclamation itself. Can we imagine, for example, going through the four Gospels and snipping out the passages that talk about Jesus' concern for the poor and the weak? Mark's Gospel, which has fewer of the sayings of Jesus than the others, would be completely denuded. No multiplication of the bread, no healings, no exorcisms—it would look pretty slim, a scanty collection of parables and the passion story. Peter's mother-in-law would stay feverish, the man with the withered hand would remain in the synagogue corner, the woman's hemorrhage would continue and the multitudes would make their way home without food, close to fainting.

The Gospel of John organizes the deeds of Jesus as "signs" that he performs to reveal who he is. After having performed a particular sign, Jesus, in John's Gospel, comments extensively on what this means in terms of himself, his heavenly Father and the way his followers are to treat each other. Take out the signs and the whole Gospel becomes unintelligible. Has not the church adopted some of these same powerful signs as a way to understand what evangelization means? The healing of the man born blind and the raising of Lazarus from the dead compose two key scripture readings during Lent as adults are preparing for entry into the church. The raising of Lazarus, which serves as a culmination of the signs

of John's Gospel, touches on so many levels of human bro-
kenness—the rescue of one from humanity's ultimate foe,
death; the restoration of a family; the power of God in
human life; the freedom of the human person from all bonds
(Lazarus is unwrapped); and the celebration of community
when Lazarus joins them at table once again.

As the raising of Lazarus brings the signs of Jesus to a
culmination, so the teaching of Jesus throughout the
Gospel is brought to a head in the farewell speech that
begins with the thirteenth chapter of John's Gospel. This,
too, is a deed—a dramatic and powerful deed. Jesus, in the
midst of the meal and his farewell message to his disciples,
takes off his outer robe and puts on an apron. Then he pro-
ceeds to wash the feet of his disciples, in spite of great protest
from his most prominent apostle, Peter. "Do you not understand what I have done for you? If I, who am servant and
Lord, wash your feet, must you not wash each other's feet as
well?" (Jn 13:14). In other words, the key to John's Gospel,
expressed as a Gospel of love, is the prophetic act of service
that Jesus gives for his followers.

Luke takes the deeds of Jesus and explicitly expands them
in a context of service and love. His are some of the most
memorable of parables and stories—the Good Samaritan, the
visit to Zacchaeus's house in which Zacchaeus promises to
give half of what he has earned to the poor, the raising of the
son of the widow at Naim, the parables about the Good
Shepherd and the lost coin, the sending of the twelve and
later the seventy-two to heal and proclaim the Good News;
they form the very character of Luke's gospel message. In
fact, Catholics today are perhaps most disquieted reading
Luke because, whatever our political or economic theories,

Luke challenges us to love the poor and to find the Gospel's meaning in them.

The unbroken teaching of the church from these gospel passages down to contemporary teachings about social action makes it clear that social action is hardly something peripheral to the meaning of the church. The Gospel demands that loving service be placed at the very core of Catholic life. That it is not explicitly so stands as a testimony to how much more we need to be converted ourselves to the Good News of Jesus Christ.

The fact is, without generous and free service to others, the Gospel is invisible. Flowing from discipleship, service and social ministry are the deepest applications of the notion of welcome. The inherent dignity of every person, arising from creation and redemption, means that every person should receive what human nature needs—food, shelter, family, community, education, work and wages, and the essential elements of human health.

Catholic social ministry fundamentally invites people to the table that God has set for us in creation. It insists that everyone has a space at that table, and that no one can be excluded without putting at risk every human being. This hospitality, modeled after the way Jesus accepted and addressed every person, comes with a deep sense of caring for the needs of the other person.

Sometimes Catholics talk as if there were no connection between social service to others and spreading the Gospel. True enough, often Catholics seem more ready to serve another's need than to share the Good News with them—certainly a distortion that needs to be corrected. Yet all the narration of scriptural stories will mean nothing without the witness of serving another primarily out of love for the other. Such hospitality, such witness, can become the framework for invitation and proclamation. Unless people feel welcomed into the human network of believers with their dignity upheld, it will be almost impossible to invite them into the faith of those believers.

In Our Parishes

Parishioners rally to nothing more clearly than vividly dramatized human need. We can talk theory and theology, we can claim great causes and propose sweeping denunciations. None of that will have the direct appeal of simply presenting the human and spiritual needs of others to our congregations. And the responses of our congregations will come in two forms: They will write checks and, if it is made convenient for them, they will volunteer to serve.

Witness for example:

- The growing contributions to the Campaign for Human Development.
- The response to the clearly presented needs of aging nuns and brothers.
- The donations of money and clothing during crises and tragedies.
- The dozens of people in thousands of parishes who sign up to serve in the shelters or the soup kitchens that parishes sponsor or support.
- The numerous social justice committees in Catholic parishes throughout the United States.
- The thousands of believers who support and are involved with Pax Christi.

- The prevalence of the St. Vincent de Paul Society, particularly in those parishes that serve the poorest populations.

While instances of these kinds of generous responses abound in our parish life, there are plenty of other examples that show how hard it is for parishes to respond in the ways of Christ.

Scene 1: The Social Action Committee of the parish has organized a Thursday soup kitchen, in which people can come, feel welcomed, have some hearty soup and bread and receive a small bag of food supplies for later use. However, every Friday morning the women's guild comes in, never finds the kitchen up to par and complains without fail to the pastor.

Scene 2: A request for help comes in to the St. Vincent de Paul Society. Even though the need is vividly presented, the members feel obliged to analyze whether the family is "truly" poor and to make clear that, being helped this once, they should not expect more help in the future.

Scene 3: A parish has worked hard to organize outreach to youth in its area, youth particularly prone to be victims of poverty, crime and drug use. The more the parish performs these actions, the more difficult it is to maintain a strong sense of order and control simply because of the problems that are being dealt with. The parents of the parish, however, some of whose children are served by the program, will not respond to requests for help. Instead, they complain about how these programs are taking away from their own feeling of being served.

Scene 4: An urban parish reluctantly responds to the city's request that it help care for the homeless. Part of its reluctance has to do with a feeling of colluding with the failure of a city to respond to real housing needs through a Band-Aid approach. However, it begins a very successful ministry to the homeless. After three years it dawns on one of the organizers that of all the people welcomed into the church's basement to sleep on a cot, not one has been invited to take a seat in a pew on Sunday.

Readers can probably recall scenes from their own experience that mirror the above. These and other scenes show that it is in the parish's actual ministry, in its very activity, that its commitment to the service of others is verified. Talk all it wants, only the actual deeds of a parish, only the concrete gestures of service, speak clearly to the issue. Inversely, the concrete ignoring of human needs speaks clearly about unchristian and even immoral attitudes that still maintain a place in our imaginations and obscure the Gospel's proclamation.

Vanquishing these attitudes until we have put on the mind of Christ as revealed in the Gospels, both personally and as parish communities, remains one of the key evangelization agendas of the church.

An Evangelizing Ministry

When the bishops of the United States published their plan and strategy for evangelization, *Go and Make Disciples*, they insisted that the service of others be an intrinsic part of the plan. The third of three goals that the plan places before American Catholics speaks directly to the social ministry of the Catholic parishes and people. It calls upon all of us to bring the impact of our gospel beliefs into the world, into the social structures of society, in order to shape a complete image of what evangelization means for Catholics. It goes on to explain how these gospel values become concrete: in our concern for the poor, the family, the common good and every person entitled by his or her very existence to human dignity.

The social ministry of the church should be understood, therefore, as an inherently evangelizing activity, just as the deeds of Jesus were integrated into his teaching and message. The inclusion of the third goal in the bishops' plan stands as a challenge to Catholic parishes in two ways: by moving their ministries of service more clearly to the center of the parish's life and by viewing these ministries as directly related to everything else the parish does as part of its evangelizing activity.

Obviously, when we hear about the inherent dignity of every person and addressing the human needs of the poor, we can become paralyzed by the very magnitude of the task before us. What are we supposed to do with all these poor people? Or all the addicted? Or all these immigrants? Or all the sick?

The key to this ministry has always been to organize concrete activities that begin to address these needs in practical, realistic ways. Doing this is to engage in prophetic activity. After all, did Jesus cure every sick or leprous person in Palestine while he lived? Did Jesus radically change the political or economic structure of his society? Of course not. His actions were undertaken as prophetic signs of the kingdom of God that he had come to proclaim and bring about. In our own ministry, this double focus of Jesus cannot be forgotten. Our deeds are important in themselves, but their deeper religious meaning lies in their proclamation of a new vision of human life that God wants to bring about.

Consequently, parishes have to be willing to engage in the planning necessary to translate large visions into particular action-steps. Inadequate as it will always be, parishes have to look at what is around them and begin to address needs that their world undeniably presents. Whether a wealthy parish in a growing suburb or an impoverished parish in a forgotten part of the inner city, each must adopt the concrete steps by which it dares, in the Spirit of Jesus, to approach the lowly of today.

What happens when parishes humbly approach those deemed lowly in society? Nothing less than the beginning of an evangelizing encounter because, in order to do so, parishes will need to lay aside their own images and be willing to encounter "the other" for their very inherent value. In such exchanges, as the life of Jesus demonstrates, the kingdom of God begins to appear.

The very first image that has to be laid aside is that of looking down on "the other" because they do not immediately fit into the social image of the parishioners. To patronize is not to meet another, not to engage them heart-to-heart, not to sit down at table with them. To patronize is to raise a protective filter between ourselves and "the other" in order to maintain our self-justifying vision intact.

The next image that disappears is the one that seduces us into thinking that we already have everything or know everything. To engage the other is to be drawn into the world of that other, the different perspectives and emphases, the varying relationships and values. These disrupt our self-satisfied poses as much as any parable in the Gospels.

A third image that also has to vanish involves the narcissistic one that "we come first," because when we serve others it means that we have to die and rise, we have to put the other first, we have to bend down with the "apron of the Lord" and "wash the feet" of others. This amounts to a spiritual purification in which we come to see others as equals, even though, by society's standards, no equality exists.

A fourth image also has to be set aside as a result of coming to see all others as our equals. That is the seductive image that "we have everything to give and nothing to receive." When parishes truly engage the needy, they receive the Gospel in new and powerful ways. When parishes truly encounter the other, they become the gospel communities they are called to be. Compare, for example, a parish's view of itself before and after it has been called upon to welcome an immigrant community. Such a parish has been forced to give up being a "club" (an all-too-natural pattern) and experience what it means to be "community."

A fifth image called into question, one common in the middle and upper classes of both the Depression generation and the baby boomers, concerns insufficiency. No matter how much security they have, it is not enough; no matter how much food, how adequate their housing and clothing, no matter how wonderful their vacations—they never have enough. There is a basic obsession with accumulation.

Setting aside such images means that the parish goes through a conversion experience, a death and resurrection in which it has entered in trust into a future that it resisted— and found new life by taking that step. At the same time, encountering "the other" will involve a stark invitation to death and resurrection, as the poor and needy have to lay aside their defenses, their destructive ways of coping and hiding, and face a more explicit uncovering of the Gospel.

Doing the Ministry

A parish has various ways of doing deeds of justice, love and peace that characterize the kingdom of God. Unfortunately, these deeds often remain in the hands of a few dedicated people, and parishes themselves, as communities, are not usually challenged to engage in the social ministry of Good News for the world except through financial contributions. One of the key agenda items for pastors and pastoral leaders lies exactly in this area: extending the sense of the church's social ministry in such a way that the whole parish sees it as the community's responsibility.

Parishes generally let the social ministry default to:

- The St. Vincent de Paul Society
- The social justice committee
- Youth preparing for confirmation
- The social action coordinator
- The local interfaith liaison
- Those who work in shelters, soup kitchens or other programs to address social crises

How can these and other interested parishioners bring an evangelizing dimension to their ministry? Here are some principles and approaches.

1. *Develop direct contacts with those in need.*

Evangelization occurs through human encounter and, sad to say, people generally resist contact with those who are needy. They grow comfortable with their own social worlds and shun any intrusions into those worlds, particularly from anyone who would threaten them. This protective pattern can exist even in the inner city, where certain people see themselves as a class different from their surrounding neighbors.

Yet only by direct contact with people whose needs expose the social facades and masks that obscure the Gospel can the Good News begin to be more clearly proclaimed. The very protective screen that we use to keep people at a distance has to be broken down if the power of the Gospel will be known.

Those in need either exist within the parish or, if one's community is an enclave, in other parts of the local area. Ministers need to dare to encounter these needy people to see what the Spirit would bring about.

2. *Listen as you meet.*

With dialogue and interchange, ministers have an opportunity to listen to the depths of those God gives us to encounter. This listening has to happen on many levels. Of course, the overt needs of others have to be addressed, as St. James warned us when he wrote that it made little sense to greet others and leave them hungry (Jas 2:14–16). But these overt needs often betoken covert needs and often the most pressing of human needs, that of human and spiritual contact. Ministers evangelize by their presence and their capacity to listen.

3. *Create community.*

Through engaging and listening, a community begins to be built, one in which all come to be seen as brothers and sisters, erasing the poverty marker that we often use to tag another person. The inherent dignity of each person gives them an entrée to a universal world composed of that fraternity which characterizes the kingdom of God. In Christ there are no haves and have-nots. There are only brothers and sisters in community.

4. *Appropriately challenge people to renewal and conversion.*

The use of the word *appropriately* is of capital importance since it is not the nature of God's love to hold people in need hostage to a succession of homilies. Yet the deeds that we do in the name of Christ call for the kingdom to be the context of our actions. While Jesus did not demand faith in order to heal people and, in fact, often had table fellowship with the scorned of society, the context of his whole ministry was to call people to a renewed understanding of themselves in relation to God and to a change of heart. This change might come in a variety of forms (pardon, restoration, inclusion, hope, care for others, as a few examples) because the kingdom of God does not come in only one package or through only one unnuanced message.

The appropriate call to renewal and conversion means that we do not hold our faith over people as some kind of stick or some kind of superior platform making them feel even worse about themselves. *Appropriately* means relying on love, our belief in human dignity, plain human courtesy and socially contextualized moments to invite others to new opportunities in their lives. Obviously, we come to know these appropriate moments only when we have formed a community of love.

The call to conversion just as obviously comes to the minister him- or herself. God calls all to change. God calls all to renewed relationships. Those who are served also call us at appropriate moments of our ministry to change and renewal. Ministers cannot undertake this work in the name of Christ without a willingness to undergo profound change themselves.

5. *Make your community known through invitation.*

One way to help others know your community is by

including them in it. As people have contact with us, as they feel genuine love that affirms the parity of all as children in the kingdom of God, they can hear more clearly words of invitation to partake of dimensions of our parish life. For example, it may be difficult for some people to feel at ease in our fancy church naves; but initially they may feel much more at ease at parish picnics, dinners, social events and education programs. Children in shelters, for example, are often the last ones to be welcomed into a catechetical program or into a summer vacation bible school. Yet when the poor begin to have this kind of contact and are not made to feel self-conscious, they can begin to hear other invitations and, over time, come to see the faith community as their own.

6. *Look at immediate needs, particularly family needs.*

Often the greatest social needs cut across social and demographic lines. Family needs are a good example of this. Although it plays out differently in the world of malls than in the world of street corners, stresses today test all families. Social ministers can help everyone in the parish by creating ways to address these familial needs—interpersonal communication; loneliness; domestic violence; care for the elderly; economic hardship; the particular needs of youth, the elderly, the separated and divorced, recovery groups or single parents; the place of work (or, more likely, overwork) in the family's life; attitudes toward basic life issues; parenting skills and other questions that plague families today.

In attending to basic family needs, care has to be taken not to seem to exclude those who are single and who often feel they have no place in today's parishes. If the depth of needs are read correctly, then all parishioners will feel some kinship with these family initiatives.

7. *Don't overlook education.*

Catholics today, particularly in North America, are oblivious to their social power. They still live as if they were a besieged population, a persecuted minority, unable to do much but survive. Such images of Catholics, even taking into account the large immigration of people from the Latin and Asian worlds, simply do not work today. Most Catholics are highly educated and are therefore in a position to be informed and aware of social and public issues—matters that should concern them greatly.

Why are our parishes not forums of dialogue about media, public issues, governmental objectives, educational values, labor relationships, workplace values and faith, church-and-state issues, and public values? The estimated sixty-plus million Catholics in the United States today should be having a much greater impact on our world than they do. Parish ministers can help provoke these discussions and provide venues where they can take place. Additionally, they can help direct any resolutions that emerge from these dialogues to some kind of proper action.

8. *Empower laypeople to be disciples.*

A final direction that social ministers can take lies in the area of helping laypeople be the disciples that they are. While the church can offer general principles and articulate fundamental values, only laypeople, who have the experience of being "in the world"—in the home, the neighborhood, the workplace and the larger society—can really work out in the concrete what these values mean.

Ministers in the parish can help laypeople have voice—professionals, educators, financiers, blue-collar workers, medical personnel, legal professionals, practitioners of the various forms of modern media and all the other avenues of commerce and public discourse that make up today's world.

Only when the Gospel becomes second nature to Catholics exercising their place in the world will the Good News begin to penetrate the modern world as it was meant to be.

Although it takes on a dramatically different shape than many other ministries, the underlying evangelical power present in all ministry shows itself through the same gospel dynamics. Disciples committed to love Christ and "the other" in Christ's name, reach out to those whom Christ loved in a special way—the poor, marginalized and isolated. That outreach forms what is perhaps the most extreme example of hospitality that Christians can show, making space for those who have no space, embracing those considered least likely to be embraced. This is done for the sake of the love of the other, out of acknowledgment for the inherent dignity God has given everyone. But it also constitutes the witness of deeds that must accompany the proclamation of God's Word. It also leads to invitation and proclamation when community has been built enough that others can come to see themselves around the Lord's table, eager to hear God's Word.

If evangelization would change the world, it must have a strong social mission.

Reflecting on Our Ministry

• Who are most readily welcomed into our parish community and who are most ignored?
• Who in my parish community responds to the needs of those who have the least? How widespread is the mission to

care for others? What are the most obvious ministries that show the parish's commitment to the poor and needy?

• How does my involvement in this ministry show hospitality, invitation, witness, care for others and invitation into community?

• What kinds of gifts do the poorest bring to me and my parish? What kinds of gifts do I and my parish bring to the poor?

• How does my ministry preserve the dignity of each person that is served? How does my parish community avoid patronizing or pitying those in need?

• What kind of welcome do the poor get at the rectory? Are they ever present in the congregation on Sunday? Are there subtle or overt class divisions in my parish community?

• What kinds of personal relationships do I form in my social ministry commitment? What kinds of personal bonds do I form with others, particularly the stranger?

• How often does my parish reflect on the social teaching of the church? How would my parish react to most of that teaching?

• How do I bring a more conscious evangelizing framework to the social ministry that I do?

CHAPTER ELEVEN

Evangelizing the Bereaved

On this mountain the Lord of hosts will make for all peoples a feast of rich food, a feast of well-aged wines, of rich food filled with marrow, of well-aged wines strained clear. And he will destroy on this mountain the shroud that is cast over all peoples, the sheet that is spread over all nations; he will swallow up death forever.

Isaiah 25:6–7 NRSV

For months they knew it was coming. Slowly the cancer grew in their mother's frame and no amount of chemotherapy could hold it back. From soft tissue to bone, from important organs to vital ones, the doctors narrated the pace of the disease.

When death did come, it struck the children in ways they did not expect. Of course they knew the tears would come, the remorse and endless thoughts about "what else we could have done," and the flood of memories from various episodes in life that fixed the image of mother in the minds of each of her children. All that they expected.

What they did not expect was the resurgence of questions about faith because, although their mother was a believing and practicing Catholic, much of her prayer life centered around praying for her children's return to the practice of their faith. But as they saw the neighborhood priest and eucharistic ministers visit their mother over the months, and when they sat with the funeral director talking about the funeral, when they had to face how they would celebrate the memory of their mother, it became clear to them that she could not be understood apart from her faith. And that faith had to be part of her farewell. This meant that they would have to look at faith in their own lives once again.

Their mother was evangelizing them even beyond death, and that process would continue with the help of committed believers long after their mother was buried.

When a death occurs in a family, along with the great sadness and mourning there are powerful opportunities to evangelize. For Catholics, just like anyone else, death becomes a test of faith, wherein the survivors sort through the questions of life's purpose and meaning. Do we truly believe in resurrection? Do we believe life comes through death? What do we think the death of a carpenter two thousand years ago has to do with the lifeless corpse of one we love? Should we have expected more out of life, or did we expect too much?

This process of sorting out life's questions is not easy. Some Catholics may easily be able to say, "Oh, of course we believe in life ever after! That's what we have always been taught!" For others, though, it's not so easy. A myriad of serious, critical questions arise, not just about everlasting life but about God's will, power and love.

Quite often believers offer words of consolation in language like: "It was God's will...." But behind our facile use of this kind of consolation, what beliefs do people really hold? What are we making of God when we presume to know God's will? It is not, in any compelling sense, God's will for a five-year-old to run out into the street and be killed by a drunk driver. It is not God's will for a father of young children to be shot and killed in an attempted burglary. It is not God's will for a fifty-five-year-old woman to succumb to lung cancer after smoking all of her life. It is not the will of God for an eighteen-year-old to put a gun to his head and pull the trigger. It is not God's will for a forty-year-old to die a long, lingering death.

In fact, in all of these cases, God probably did not have anything directly to do with these events. These are the results of decisions we make for ourselves (such as smoking) or the result of decisions that other people make over which we have no control (the decision to drink and drive, the decision to rob a store at gunpoint) or the consequences of forces intertwined with the evolution of nature. Even a natural death of an elderly person, for example, is not necessarily "the direct will of God," but instead the result of the natural process of aging.

We Catholics read as part of the regular lectionary cycle that "God did not make death and takes no delight in the death of anyone," from the Book of Wisdom (1:13). In spite of this truth, we continue to make God the "fall guy" for all of life's difficulties.

The Many Reactions to Death

Death and suffering have many different faces, so the death experience will be different for each of the survivors. Despite these variations, it is pretty certain that all of the surviving members of the family, close friends and significant others will enter into a state of shock—if not immediately, then at some proximate time.

Many people, upon learning of the serious, life-threatening or terminal illness of a loved one, enter into shock immediately and begin to experience the grieving process even while their loved one is still alive. They are numb and often confused, but manage to keep going on a strong flow of activity and adrenaline. Visiting the hospital at all hours of the day, making arrangements for distant family members to visit, assisting other family members to cope with the suffering their loved one may be experiencing—in all of this, they are trying to cope themselves. The busyness helps the process. In long, drawn-out cases, there are often decisions to be made—moving the patient to another medical facility or hospice, trying new treatments and other life-and-death medical decisions. Still, the coping continues.

In many of these cases, even though the medical reality is pronounced as terminal, incurable or inoperable, hope still surges in the human heart. While there's life, there's hope. The friends and relatives of the patient hold onto a thin thread of hope, even as they watch their loved one deteriorate. They are in shock and denial, both before and after the death—the shock and denial contrasting directly with their irrepressible hope.

In other cases, death comes with no advance notice. Hope does not even have time to emerge from the human heart, which is stunned by the sudden phone call, the unexpected incident, the unforeseen heart attack or the rage of modern violence. Denial has little wiggle-room in these situations; it quickly yields to shock and then often to anger.

It has often been debated whether it is easier to lose a loved one after a long illness or suddenly, through a catastrophic event such as a heart attack, an accident or a crime. Neither situation is easy. The benefit of having the opportunity to say good-bye in the first case is negated by the suffering of the person who is dying. In the case of a sudden death, especially when there is little or no suffering, this consolation is overturned by not having a chance to say good-bye, to reconcile, make amends or let someone know just how very much they have meant.

A minister to the bereaved must be aware of the many different reactions that may occur after a death of a loved one and must be able to respond to a wide variety of emotions. Even with the death of the same person, different survivors may react quite differently—one with anger and rage, one with profound sadness, one with deep depression, one with guilt and regrets, one with relief.

To serve the bereaved is to empathize with the grieving, that is, to be willing to share with another a whole range of reactions to death's unfriendly face, whether it shows itself slowly over time or "like a thief in the night."

Ideal Bereaved Ministry

In some parishes, the role of the minister to the bereaved is limited to the function of assisting with planning the mass or providing a reception after the funeral.

However, a more comprehensive parish ministry to the bereaved might well include many more functions.

1. Peer Ministry

The best ministers to those experiencing a sudden, unexpected death in the family are those who have experienced a similar tragedy in their own lives. Those parents, for example, who have lost children are the ideal ministers to other bereaved parents. Likewise, the widow who nursed her husband through the last months or years of his life is the perfect person to minister to another who is faced with loss through terminal illness. Accordingly, it is a benefit if the bereaved ministry committee in the parish has many kinds of survivors, those who have actually experienced the death of a loved one through a variety of illnesses—lingering illnesses such as cancer, ALS, or emphysema—as well as those who have suffered a sudden or accidental death of a loved one.

The empathy of those who have similarly suffered can only strengthen the inherent support of peer outreach.

2. Long-term Illness

In the case of long-term illness, bereavement ministry could begin well before the eventual death. Bereavement ministers need to be trained carefully in the art of listening and counseling as the family members move through this heart-rending experience.

During times of crisis, ministers might offer physical assistance, such as driving family members to the hospital, baby-sitting, shopping or providing meals. A very real service can be provided to the patients by offering them the opportunities to write or tape final messages to their family and to plan their own vigil and funeral services. If trained properly, ministers can provide a tremendous service by sensitively broaching the subjects of organ donation and living wills with the patients and their families.

It goes without saying that ministers to the bereaved in these situations need to be eucharistic ministers, bringing communion frequently to the sick and dying, praying with them and for them both publicly and privately. Spiritual books and pamphlets can be offered; spiritual tapes and CDs are also very comforting to the seriously ill. Comfort and consolation can be offered to the family members who have already begun the grieving process, mourning the loss of health and well-being of their loved one.

3. Sudden Tragedy

For those who experience sudden and unexpected loss, timing is everything. How are the members of the bereavement committee notified of the death? Does the pastor notify them immediately upon learning of the death or on being informed by the funeral home of the need for funeral arrangements? Is there a prearranged plan for bereavement members to follow in the case of sudden death? Are they trained in what to say and what not to say? What to do and what not to do?

Ideally, an initial call should be made immediately to set up an appointment for a visit as soon as possible after the death. It is too late to wait a day or two to offer assistance in planning the funeral mass or the vigil service. It is too late to offer to drive the survivors to the morgue or to the funeral home to make arrangements. It is too late to ask (if appropriate) whether the deceased's organs are to be donated. It is too late to be of assistance in making phone calls to relatives, arranging for out-of-town relatives to come, helping with meals, baby-sitting, transportation or clothing needs. The family may need immediate assistance in dealing with the police, attorneys, or victim advocates in the case of accidental or criminal deaths.

Even if the bereaved family members do not need or desire the assistance of the minister, contact from those in the bereavement ministry lets them know that the death is acknowledged and mourned by the local faith community. An offer of assistance and support, even if unaccepted, is an immeasurable gesture and will remain in the memory of the grieving.

4. Vigil Service and Funeral Mass

More and more parishes today are both simplifying and personalizing the viewing and funeral services by having afternoon visitation hours in the church, followed by the Mass of Christian Burial in the early evening. Although unheard of less than a decade ago, this new practice points back to earlier days, when the wake was held in the family parlor. Many survivors have said how appreciative they were that the funeral could be celebrated in the evening, when more friends and neighbors were able to attend. Also the survivors have the strong feeling that the death is being honored, mourned and celebrated as a parish event with the whole faith community invited to the funeral.

Whether the viewing is held in the church or in the funeral home, the minister to the bereaved, along with the pastoral ministers, is the visual sign of the support of the faith community. Without being intrusive, the minister is the liaison between the family and the community, offering his or her services to the family in the name of the local parish. Ministers to the bereaved may assist in welcoming people to the wake or the funeral, helping them to sign the guest book, distributing memorial cards and programs or attending to the needs of the family.

By this time, the minister might well have formed a personal and trusting relationship with the bereaved, through visits made before or immediately after the death or through assisting the family with funeral plans. The minister should make it known to the primary family members or friends that he or she is present and available, should the family need anything. It is not uncommon, for example, for family members, in the midst of their shock and all the details that must be attended to, to overlook mundane chores. An extra hand and a calmer spirit mean so much.

If it is the custom, the minister can arrange to have the vigil service and/or mass unobtrusively audio- or videotaped as discretely as possible. Many bereaved people often say that the funeral was "beautiful," but they cannot remember a single word of the readings or homily. They cannot remember who came to the viewing, or, because of the order of the procession at mass, they may not even know who was present at the funeral. Many report that a videotape helps them long after the funeral to remember the experience of being supported by a loving, caring community. Often, it is the knowledge of the community's support at the time of loss that sustains them through the long grieving period to follow.

A very practical and welcomed service offered by the bereavement committee, perhaps in conjunction with the women's guild, is to have a reception after the funeral and burial. This may be held in the parish hall or in the family home, but the arrangements with the family must be made ahead of time to prevent duplication. In all of this ministering around the time of the funeral, parish ministers offer themselves in service within the context of the family, its members and its resources. Ministers do not compete with the family at the time of death.

5. Bereavement Ministry

A day or two after the funeral might be a good time for another visit from the minister. Most of the distant family members have returned to their homes and the sudden quiet and lack of things to do leave the bereaved wondering "what do I do now?" After the surge of activity before the funeral, there is a letdown when it is all over and everyone has gone home. A well-timed visit, always preceded by a call, can offer the bereaved time alone with the minister without other members of the family around, to perhaps express his or her feelings more freely, to review the events of the past few days, to remember the services, to raise religious questions. Even a visit in which the minister sits with the person in silence is of tremendous value. This ministry of presence allows the bereaved to express thoughts and feelings, worries or concerns, or just to sit silently in the presence of someone who understands and cares.

As time goes on, ministry to the bereaved continues as the grieving and healing progress. A phone call or visit, a note or a card, are so appreciated by the bereaved person—especially on special occasions such as birthdays, anniversaries and holidays. The relationship between the minister and the bereaved continues, grows and is strengthened. As friendships form, the minister always attends to the needs of the bereaved—actual physical needs or needs for silence and comfort.

A minister should be able to talk with the bereaved about their loved one, mentioning him or her by name, encouraging the survivors to harvest their memories and celebrate their lives. For example, one of the tasks of a specialist in bereavement therapy is to "get to know the loved one almost as well as the survivor does." This is accomplished through talking and writing, sharing memories, reflecting upon relationships, remembering both the good and the not so good about their loved one and themselves. Another task of the therapist is to honor the feelings of the bereaved client and to assure him or her that these feelings are authentic and acceptable. When volatile emotions arise, such as guilt or anger, the bereavement specialist assists the client to accept these feelings as normal and to work through them. While ministers to the bereaved are usually not professionally trained grief therapists, it might be helpful to them to be aware of some of these tasks and to respond appropriately when the situation arises. Also, the minister may recommend grief therapy for someone who is having difficulty with the grieving process.

A minister should encourage the bereaved person to mourn, because the only way to get through grief is by going *through* grief. A person cannot bypass it or go around it or avoid it or rationalize it. Eventually, the loss must be faced and accepted in its finality, and the wounds—all the "what ifs," "should haves" and "if onlys"—must be reconciled for healing to occur. Otherwise, the body and mind can eventually react with manifestations of physical illness, depression, anxiety or other debilitating conditions. Facing death and going through grief is much harder in today's world, where death seems to happen on the video screen but not in real life.

The Evangelizing Minister of the Bereaved

Few other life events possess the opportunity for evangelization as does death. The sensitive evangelizing minister is aware of the primary opportunities for welcoming and befriending those who mourn, for witnessing and proclaiming their faith, and for inviting and integrating them into a loving, caring faith community. A secondary benefit is that the love and care that are basic prerequisites for the evangelization process are evident not only to the immediately bereaved but also to mourners attending the services or visiting the home.

The process of dying and rising, the ultimate proclamation of the Good News, arises at the time of death with an undeniable physical force. Every death challenges the disciple to reaffirm faith again. Every death causes us to sort out life's meaning and presents an opportunity to commit ourselves once again to Christ. In ministering to the bereaved, the dimensions of evangelization take on a delicate shape, but they are there nonetheless. Sensitivity to the feelings of others, witness of our faith and proclamation of the Good News through all the ceremonies surrounding death take on more power at the time of loss. Every consoling gesture contains the underlying statement of the Gospel within it. The evangelizing minister of bereavement should be keenly aware, with great humility, of the gospel power of his or her ministry.

Death brings many people back to church for the first time, possibly after many years; it is crucial that they be welcomed, comforted and consoled. Death provides an immediate and relevant opportunity for proclaiming the Christian faith. Death is the time when one's authentic and unfailing belief in the resurrection of the dead is of ultimate importance. Even if the mourner does not believe or is not sure of what he or she believes, the uncompromising proclamation of the minister's faith is not only comforting and reassuring—it is also thought-provoking. It may make the critical difference in a person's ongoing conversion process.

Through quiet assurance of hope and peace, the silent witness of the minister's faith may profoundly influence the mourners as they work through the grieving process. The invitation into an appropriate support group may be the invitation back to church that inactive or unchurched mourners need. And eventually, inviting the mourners themselves to become ministers to the bereaved, will bring the process full circle. Loving service to others will enable, strengthen and support those who, by the very nature of their loss, will continue to grieve one way or another for the rest of their lives.

Most of all, those who mourn need to know that the death of their loved one is acknowledged and honored by the faith community. Any means through which that love and compassion and caring are shown reflects the face of a loving, caring and compassionate God for those suffering their loss. "Blessed are those who mourn for they shall be consoled" (Mt 5:4).

The personal sharing of grief reflects in human dynamics the deeper theological dynamics of salvation. For how does salvation happen? When we reflect upon it through the prism of death, we understand that our human mortality and our human limitations are the boundary of human existence. Death shows our smallness, our virtual insignificance. Only when God shares this death through the dying and rising of Jesus Christ does the process of death cease to be the absolute border of human life. Rather, it transforms itself from being a border to being a doorway, an entryway into life everlasting, which was revealed by Jesus Christ in his resurrection.

God shares our death, robbing it of its power to humiliate us and restoring to our hearts the grounds of hope that seem to be embedded in the human spirit. Even stoics dare at times to dream. God, through sharing our death in Christ, pours into us the Spirit of life that Christ won in his resurrection and transfers to all those who dwell in him. As we pray in one of the prefaces for a funeral mass, "By dying, Christ destroyed our death; by rising, he gave us new life."

This fundamental Christian proclamation is heard again and again in different ways as we go through life. But it is heard with a poignancy and power most of all at times of death, particularly with the death of one most beloved. The minister, then, through the human dynamics of sharing and empathizing, helps in this saving process of appropriating the death and resurrection of Jesus into human life experience. This sharing between Christ and us, in death and resurrection, forms the basis of our claim for life eternal. We have already died in Christ; only life awaits us, if we go through the process of death with faith.

Reflecting on Our Ministry

• Do I stay current in my reading on grief management through books and magazine articles?
• Does my diocese or parish have specific training for ministers to the bereaved? How often are they offered? What can I do to help involve others in this ministry?

• Does the parish have a worksheet for vigil services and funeral masses? Am I familiar enough with the liturgy to assist the bereaved in planning these services?

• Do I have the support I need in doing this ministry? Who supports me and helps me keep perspective?

• Do I remember to pray often for the bereaved? For other ministers to the bereaved?

• Is there an educational process in the parish (before tragedies occur) for informing and assisting people, as death approaches, regarding funeral preparation, organ donation or living wills?

• How can I actualize further the potential impact of invitation and renewal in faith among the bereaved and those attending the services?

CHAPTER TWELVE

Working with the Clergy

*What identifies our priestly service, gives a profound unity
to the thousand and one tasks which claim our attention
day by day and throughout our lives, and confers a distinct
character on our activities, is this aim, ever present in
all our action: to proclaim the Gospel of God.*
On Evangelization in the Modern World, #68

Of all the questions parishioners ask in the field of
evangelization, none is as overworked as this: "How do I
get my pastor to be interested in evangelization?" Or on a
higher level, "How do we wake up these bishops?" Hardly a
conference or workshop on evangelization is given without
an earnest participant desperately asking questions like
these.

Desperate is the word. Once people have it in their hearts
to spread the Good News, once they have caught the fire
of the Gospel, which naturally wants to spread, nothing
frustrates laypersons more than having the clergy leadership tell them to douse the flame or otherwise contain
their burning desire. Such people, seeking to work in and

for the church, are so frustrated that they feel desperate. *Desperate* is close in meaning to "dispirited" and "without hope." These lay men and women had hoped to work for the Gospel but now have to bide their time or even reverse the strides that they've made in their life of discipleship.

It is our observation that clergy—bishops, priests and deacons—are more and more disposed toward evangelization. We have seen a substantial shift in the attitude of clergy in the past ten years. However many exploding parishes or populated churches may exist in an area, all bishops and priests know many more parishes whose pews are almost empty and whose activities never transcend the routine. No ordained person can ignore the threats to Catholic life and identity that we pointed out in the first chapter of this book. As a result, clergy are concerned about church membership, church involvement and the growth of their congregations in discipleship. They are well aware of the permeable world of young people, where switching churches or simply not attending church are ready options. They deal with the migration of new peoples with new gifts to the local churches across the United States and Canada; they look for tools to serve and involve these new people.

As a result, bishops, priests and deacons today are playing an ever greater role in the emergence of the "new springtime of evangelization," of which Pope John Paul II speaks. To be sure, this new role has not emerged easily. It has been a rocky road with many bumps and curves—but one that has slowly wended its way from resistance, to curiosity, to tolerance, to support, to a growing but cautious enthusiasm. Some dioceses and parishes are in the "enthusiasm mode"— it shows in the way their clergy empower the laity to evangelize. Many dioceses and parishes, however, are in the "tolerance mode." The recent great movements surrounding the millennium seem to be nudging all dioceses and parishes, willy-nilly, into the "support mode."

Gradually, it has dawned on the clergy that, in the Catholic understanding, evangelization has to be rooted in the ministries that are the stock in trade of the ordained—Word and sacrament. Evangelization has been demystified by years of reflection. It no longer seems to be the unusual behavior of overly enthused people, but rather the ordinary behavior of the church, done by all who consider themselves disciples. As false images of evangelization have been discarded, new images of evangelization based on the catechumenate and the peer outreach dynamics of every parish have gradually come to take their place. Parish after parish experiences the gratifying success of receiving new members—sometimes scores of new members—into the church at the Easter Vigil. Thousands of Catholics have also made their way back to the practice of their faith through their parishes. Today as parishes experience this, they want to know how to facilitate these processes even better. Clergy have likewise seen a liturgical awakening in their parishes and have witnessed laypeople asking to explore the Word of God more deeply. They want to support and extend these avenues of renewal.

The Evangelizing Parish and the Clergy

The guiding style of working with the clergy, whether bishop, priest or deacon, is collaboration. The U.S. bishops, in their plan and strategy for evangelization, *Go and Make Disciples*, explicitly challenge the clergy to collaborate with laypersons in this ministry for the obvious reason that spreading the Gospel involves what goes on inside and beyond the church walls. The bishops say, "Evangelization must be seen as a *collaborative* effort that springs from a partnership between the clergy and the laity. Priests have a special leadership role in carrying out this plan, but they should not feel isolated, overburdened or frustrated in implementing it [italics in original]." The single cause for the clergy's hope is their collaboration with laypersons in reflecting on, planning for and executing evangelizing activities.

Behind every evangelizing lay minister stands an evangelizing bishop. Behind every evangelizing parish stands an evangelizing pastor. And within every effective evangelizing parish stands a strong group of committed laypersons who see themselves as empowered disciples. An evangelizing pastor or pastoral administrator, by definition, represents the parish. And the parish, by definition, is composed of evangelizing laypersons serving in a variety of ministries.

All too often, as the pastor goes, so goes the parish. Because priests have a special leadership role in evangelization, their impact, positive or negative, can be decisive. It is virtually impossible to have an evangelizing parish without an evangelizing pastor who not only embraces the vital evangelizing dimensions in his own ministry but enables and empowers others in the parish by providing encouragement, training and resources. However, sometimes a pastor is only interested in maintaining the status quo in the parish, building new facilities or refurbishing old ones, and raising funds to maintain the present facility or school. In these cases, the outreach dimension of evangelization will be harder to see. If the pastor is burned out, exhausted or ill, he simply will not have the energy to evangelize.

Collaboration in the pastoral realities of today's church recognizes that pastors (and bishops) have tremendous responsibilities arising from the care of those who are already committed to the faith. Accordingly, if evangelizing lay ministers desire a life-giving, worshiping community, they must assume some of those responsibilities by supporting and assisting their ordained ministers. Likewise, the ordained must be open to receiving support, considering new ideas and enabling lay ministry.

The more clergy are aware of the gospel dynamics in their own ministry, the more comfortable they can be with evangelization—both their own efforts and their own espousal of the efforts of laypeople. Every ministry touched upon in this book belongs in its first instance—but not exclusively—to the ordained. Greeting and welcoming, gathering around the table, proclaiming and feeding with the body and blood of Christ, teaching God's Word, reaching out to youth and the needy, caring for those who mourn—these functions that laypeople have rightly assumed belong also to the clergy.

As we have seen the dimensions of evangelization elaborated through a variety of lay ministries, we also can see them located in the ministry of the ordained priest. His sense of discipleship, his ability to welcome in hospitality, to set a high tone for witness and to proclaim boldly, to care for others and to bring them into community also correspond to these evangelizing dimensions in all of lay ministry.

An ordained person embodies the paschal mystery in his life for the sake of the church and the world. The paschal mystery, the ultimate evangelizing power of God, is structured into the life of the clergyman by the "character" (or indelible mark) of ordination. The character is nothing else than a configuring to the person of Christ through life and ministry "as servant and shepherd" in service of others, as Pope John Paul II teaches in *I Will Give You Shepherds*. Even in his failings, the ordained remains a paschal sign of the One who died and rose. All Christians undergo the paschal mystery of dying and rising; the ordained person does so as a public person, becoming himself a sacramental sign.

Today the ordained minister is coming more and more to see parishes as communities of ministry and communities of ministers because of the baptismal pattern of dying and rising that underlies the spiritual life of all the baptized and marks them (through receiving their baptismal "character") as disciples. Ordination builds upon baptism. As a result, we can rethink parishes as communities of disciples, all baptized into the risen Christ and empowered by Christ's Spirit. The priest's ministry, then, is paradigmatic of the ministry of everyone in the parish. He is a model, but an empowering model. His ministry ideally serves the ministries of all.

As the various lay ministries have emerged with greater clarity in the past thirty years, they have heightened the image of parish as that community where brothers and sisters share their gifts in service to each other and to the world. Paul generously castigated his Corinthian community for their spirit of contentiousness and jealousy (1 Cor 1:10 ff.). The gifts poured upon the parish today, upon the ordained and lay servants of Christ, should hardly be a cause for jealousy, conflict or division. They are, rather, the bases for collaboration.

Thinking of the parish as a community of disciples provides a framework for laypersons to work with clergy and for clergy to bless the gifts and ministries of their lay collaborators. Working with the clergy means that laypeople understand the special role of the clergy in parish life, but that they prevent that role from becoming isolated or distant. They do this by seeing their own ministries, both on and off church property, as complementing the ministry of the ordained. Personal support of the pastor helps diminish any sense of threat and provides the human context for sharing ministerial gifts. When laypeople see evangelization lying at the heart of the priest's life, and when priests see evangelization as central to what God calls the parish to be, then the foundation of collaboration between clergy and laypeople has been laid.

The evangelizing heart of Jesus Christ, then, is the norm for anyone configured in his ministry. The sacraments most associated with evangelization—baptism, confirmation, eucharist and reconciliation—structure the very ministry of the ordained. These same sacraments also structure the life and ministry of the layperson.

The Bishops and Evangelization

Neither parishes nor clergy exist in a vacuum. They are part of the local church, which is the more precise name for *diocese* in Catholic vocabulary. So the role of the bishop in modeling and stimulating evangelizing activities in the local church can hardly be ignored. It is decisive. Although the bishop cannot evangelize his whole diocese by himself, the bishop, surrounded by his presbyters and deacons, and in collaboration with committed laypeople, can bring about a dramatically different attitude among Catholics toward living and sharing their faith.

The bishops have even gone on record in support of evangelization, pledging themselves to advance its ministry. In publishing *Go and Make Disciples: A National Plan and Strategy for Catholic Evangelization in the United States* in 1993, they deliberately issued a pastoral action document to help bring about evangelizing activities among all Catholics in the United States. But they did more—they made specific promises themselves. After outlining thirty-one specific objectives, along with a myriad of possible strategies to fulfill each objective, the bishops concluded that plan by writing about their own role in implementing the strategy:

> Because this plan must involve every one of us, *we bishops first of all pledge to implement it ourselves.* We pledge, as shepherds of God's people, to proclaim the Good News of Jesus Christ through welcome, mercy and renewal. *We pledge to continue being evangelized* by the Gospel of Jesus as we meet him in our people and the challenges of today's world.
>
> We commit ourselves *to adding new full-time staff for evangelization* at the National Conference of Catholic Bishops in Washington, D.C., to help dioceses and other church agencies carry out the goals of this plan and strategy. As pastors of local churches, we realize that individuals and parishes also need support at the diocesan level. Each bishop will *seriously consider establishing a diocesan office and evangelization committee* or otherwise assign staff to give the ministry of evangelization proper visibility and attention, as well as provide resources for evangelization to his people. Parishes will be looking to these offices for direction and materials....Bishops should *take every occasion to speak out on the need and duty of every Catholic to be an evangelizer.* (Emphasis added.)

In saying this, the bishops have given us a gauge for their own commitment to evangelization, and therefore a gauge for the commitment of the clergy and the wider church to spreading the Gospel in our society.

So how's the scorecard? Have the bishops fulfilled their promises?

Promise #1: "...[W]e bishops first of all pledge to implement it ourselves. We pledge, as shepherds of God's people, to proclaim the Good News of Jesus Christ through welcome, mercy and renewal." The bishops are implementing the plan in a variety of creative ways on the diocesan level, utilizing many of the dynamics connected with the new millennium to stimulate interest. Many dioceses, with considerable commitment, have adopted three-year renewal programs such as *Renew 2000* (which reemphasizes in a new way many of the renewal and evangelizing actions of the original *Renew*), the Paulists' *Disciples in Mission* (which specifically addresses the implementation of the bishops' document), or the National Pastoral Life Center's *Follow Me* (which makes discipleship and planning the heart of parish vision). Additionally, more and more diocesan or state conferences on evangelization are being organized; more diocesan evangelization plans are being developed and implemented; and it appears that the bishops, for the most part, have turned from any initial resistance and suspicion of lay involvement.

Promise #2: "We pledge to continue being evangelized by the Gospel of Jesus as we meet him in our people and the challenges of today's world." Are the bishops continuing to be evangelized themselves? Just to publicly state before the church that ongoing conversion is an essential dimension of their episcopal ministry, the bishops have gone far in fulfilling this pledge. Evangelization and conversion continue to be on the agenda of their meetings, conferences and collective retreats. There are very good reasons, then, to take this promise at face value.

Promise #3: "...[T]o add...new full-time staff for evangelization at the National Conference of Catholic Bishops in Washington, D.C., to help dioceses and other church agencies carry out the goals of this plan and strategy." This pledge has also been accomplished, with the hiring of full-time personnel to staff the bishops' Committee on Evangelization and serve in the national office of missions. Initial results achieved by the office include the publishing of a *National Directory of Diocesan Directors of Evangelization and Contact People* and *Guidelines for Diocesan Evangelization Committees*, a helpful guide for dioceses with existing or future offices. Other documents to help with evangelization, such as guides for the ministry to inactive Catholics, will continue to appear.

Promise #4: "Each bishop will seriously consider establishing a diocesan office and evangelization committee or otherwise assign staff to give the ministry of evangelization proper visibility and attention, as well as provide resources for evangelization to his people." According to the November 1997 *National Directory of Diocesan Directors of Evangelization and Contact People* compiled by the NCCB Committee on Evangelization, there are fifty-one "directors or coordinators of evangelization," in addition to many more diocesan designates for evangelization who are variously listed as directors of religious education, spirituality, pastoral services, *Renew* or other various diocesan offices. Some of these directors are priests who wear several hats in their dioceses. Based on this information, it is difficult to ascertain exactly how many of the 177 Latin-rite dioceses in the United States now actually have full-time diocesan evangelization directors. However, with a total of 184 diocesan evangelization designates listed in the *Directory*, it appears that there is definitely an awareness or consciousness for the need of diocesan evangelization leadership that did not exist even a few years ago. Again, the evidence gives much reassurance.

Promise #5: "Bishops should take every occasion to speak out on the need and duty of every Catholic to be an evangelizer." In the early years, *evangelization* was a buzz word limited mostly to chanceries and rectories, but it now seems to have taken on new meaning and has become more and more a household word for active Catholics. While it still may be a red-flag word for some, many lay Catholics now seek understanding and growth in how evangelization integrates with their personal lives and ministries. Nearly every speech given by bishops today, reported in the Catholic press, emphasizes the need and duty of all Catholics to be evangelizers. Today's widespread familiarity with the term in Catholic circles represents a tremendous leap of awareness, understanding, knowledge and usage.

Our overwhelming impression is that working with the clergy on both the parish and diocesan levels will have less friction and more collaboration in the future. Our review of the bishops' promises and their fulfillment indicates that the measure of evangelization is quite positive. Of course, all of this is only rudimentary and preparatory at this point. The cumulative power of sixty million committed Catholics living and sharing their faith has hardly been realized. But the groundwork for such a realization has been laid.

With the growth of a sense of discipleship, and the attendant evangelizing attitudes, Catholics need no longer sigh in frustration. Our mouths, rather, are ready to gape in wonder.

Reflecting on Our Ministry

• Do I see specific, concrete actions being taken in my diocese/parish to implement the U.S. bishops' document on evangelization?

• Do I sense that the clergy in my diocese/parish are personally being evangelized? How do I help further the deepening of the Gospel's power in their lives?

• Have I noticed a change in how open the clergy are in their opinions, attitudes and behaviors concerning evangelization?

• Do I feel that the ministry of evangelization in my diocese/parish has the "proper visibility and attention" mentioned in the bishops' document?

• Does my diocese/parish provide good resources for evangelization for its members? Have a director of evangelization? Have an evangelization office or committee? Provide evangelization training for all Catholics?

• Do the clergy of this diocese/parish—bishops, priests and deacons—speak out regularly on the need and duty of every Catholic to be an evangelizer?

• Is my diocese/parish prepared to serve a larger membership when the evangelization efforts start to produce visible results?

• How do I support the clergy in my diocese? How do I help them be better evangelizers?

• How often do ideas of competition and jealousy cloud relations between clergy and laypeople, or between some clergy members and others, particularly in evangelizing activities?

• Is collaboration a hallmark of all diocesan/parish ministry?

AFTERWORD

The Most Reverend William R. Houck,
Bishop of Jackson
Former Chair,
NCCB Evangelization Committee

Years ago, I had the privilege and good fortune to meet Father Alvin Illig, C.S.P. when I was a priest in the Diocese of Birmingham. He helped me catch the flame of enthusiasm for evangelization, and I will forever be in his debt for that. In fact, many of us are indebted to that wonderful man for the same reason.

But twenty-three years after the magnificent document of Pope Paul VI, On Evangelization in the Modern World, we still struggle as Catholics with the concept, the activity and the ministry of evangelization. For you who have just finished reading *Lay Ministers, Lay Disciples,* you can count yourself among those whose struggle is succeeding! Even if you had some familiarity with Catholic evangelization, you now have more exciting insights and more practical applications of the many ways that parishioners are given the opportunity to be involved in evangelization—the essential mission of the church.

In fact, it is more than an invitation. If we are truly fully initiated Catholics, and if we claim to be disciples of Jesus Christ, then that "invitation" must become an imperative in our lives if we are to be genuine and honest about discipleship.

We can be encouraged by contributions such as this book that there is a growing awareness among more Catholics of not only the term *evangelization,* but of the fact that evangelization is "the essential mission of the church." Pope Paul VI, in his great "magna carta" of Catholic evangelization put it very clearly: "We wish to confirm once more that the task of evangelizing all people constitutes the essential mission of the church" (*Evangelii Nuntiandi,* #14).

By reading this book, you have helped yourself respond to Pope Paul VI's teaching also when he stated, "The church is an evangelizer, but she begins by being evangelized herself" (#15). And that applies not only to the church as an institution, but more especially it applies to all of us as the people of God collectively and individually. We must ourselves be evangelized and make a priority of living our Catholic faith fully and sharing it freely.

Although the Pope also says that "evangelization...is a complex process made up of various elements" (#24), this book by Susan Blum Gerding, Ed.D., and Father Frank DeSiano, C.S.P., unravels some of the complexity and elaborates in simple, clear, challenging language the practical aspects for parish ministers to become and be evangelizing ministers.

The focus in this book on parish ministers "as evangelizing ministers" relates closely to the reality for us Catholics who, for the most part, experience the church on the parish level. We have many and varyingly effective programs today to make parish life more vibrant, exciting and welcoming to our people. We also find greater commitments among more people to help every Catholic understand his or her role and responsibility in the life of the church today.

Various efforts at parish renewal have raised awareness on the part of rank and file Catholics. Their active involvement in the mission of Christ through their membership in the church today is possibly a new insight or a new focus or a new priority in their lives. It is like going in for a good swim. Some people will stand around and watch or wonder, while others are enjoying the water and having fun and making a big splash. Being fully involved in parish life is not something for Catholic people to stand around and watch or wonder about. We must find ways not only to encourage, but assist and motivate more of our fully initiated Catholics to "jump into the water," not only to have fun and splash around, but to bring new life to others and to the world as Catholic evangelizers.

One of the many things I have always loved about Jesus Christ is that he did not just preach at us. Everything he calls us to do, he himself did. We, too, are called to live a life of witnessing. In fact, "the first means of evangelization is the witness of an authentically Christian life," according to Pope Paul VI.

He went on to remind us very clearly that in our contemporary, demanding society, "Modern [men and women listen] more willingly to witnesses than to teachers, and if [they do] listen to teachers, it is because they are witnesses" (#41).

At the beginning of the last decade of the twentieth century, Pope John Paul II challenged us and all the world to use the decade of the nineties as a time to develop among all Catholics an awareness of and deeper involvement in the work of Catholic evangelization. He challenged us in his appeal (As the Third Millennium Draws Near) for adequate preparation for beginning the next Christian millennium to work for a new evangelization. Now that you have read this book, use it to raise your own awareness of the many opportunities you and other parishioners have of achieving this "new evangelization." How much the world needs what Jesus Christ has to offer is fairly self-evident. You and I have the invitation, the opportunity and hopefully now a deeper commitment to use all the means possible in the increasingly vibrant parish life in our country to make our faith joyfully effective in this wonderful world God has given us.

Lest we get too focused on ourselves, let us happily and gratefully recognize the Holy Spirit. We know very well, as Pope Paul VI tells us, evangelization is the work of the Holy Spirit. May the Holy Spirit continue to rouse us, to increase our enthusiasm and promote more and more generosity that we might respond faithfully and fully to the call of our Holy Father Pope John Paul II for a new evangelization worthy of our Catholic life in the new millennium.